DARK PSYCHOLOGY AND MANIPULATION: HOW DARK PSYCHOLOGY INFLUENCES OUR THINKING AND BEHAVIOR IN ALL AREAS OF LIFE.

Practical Guide with Exercises, Methods, Strategies to Recognize and Learn How to Defend Against Manipulation.

GEORG HOFMANN

Contents

Introduction

Dark psychology and manipulation are extremely important and current topics in a world where technology and communication tools are rapidly evolving. These techniques can be used by malicious individuals to influence and control others' behavior and negatively affect mental health, interpersonal relationships, and performance in the workplace.

Dark psychology refers to a set of psychological techniques used to influence and control others' behavior. These techniques can be used in many different situations, including interpersonal relationships, work environments, and politics. Manipulation can take many forms, including emotional control, suggestive techniques, and influencing people's behavior.

The purpose of this book is to provide a deep understanding of the concepts of dark psychology and manipulation. It will explore various ways in which these techniques can be used to influence and control the behavior of others and the negative effects these techniques can have on interpersonal relationships, performance in the workplace, and mental health.

Various examples of dark psychology and manipulation in daily life will be presented, and practical exercises and tips will be provided to develop resilience and the ability to recognize and resist manipulation techniques.

The book will also examine how manipulation can negatively affect mental health, well-being, and interpersonal and social relationships. It will also explore how manipulation is used in advertising and media and how this can influence the decisions and opinions of people.

Finally, the book will provide a practical guide for preventing and defending against manipulation, offering techniques and advice for recognizing and resisting these harmful behaviors.

The ultimate goal of this book is to provide the reader with a deeper understanding of dark psychology and manipulation, as well as the tools necessary to defend against these harmful behaviors in daily life.

The book also focuses on the history of dark psychology and how this discipline has evolved over time to provide a historical perspective on these concepts. Finally, the book provides a practical guide for preventing and defending against manipulation by providing techniques and advice for recognizing and resisting these harmful behaviors. The ultimate goal of this book is to provide the reader with a deeper under-standing of dark psychology and manipulation, as well as the tools necessary to defend against these harmful behaviors in daily life.

Introduction to Dark Psychology and Manipulation

Understanding the concepts of dark psychology and manipulation is crucial to understanding these topics and their impact on daily life. Dark psychology is a discipline that studies techniques and methods to control and manipulate the emotions, thoughts, and actions of others. Manipulation, on the other hand, is using these techniques to achieve a desired outcome. These concepts are present in many everyday situations, from interpersonal relationships to the workplace, political, and media contexts. Dark psychology and manipulation can negatively affect individuals' mental health and well-being. For example, emotional manipulation can cause stress and anxiety and also affect trust and self-esteem. Manipulation can also be used to influence the opinions and decisions of people, as in advertising or the media. Despite these negative effects, society often portrays dark psychology and manipulation positively. For example, manipulation is often seen as an important skill for personal and professional success, and dark psychology is considered an art that can be used to bring out the best in oneself and others.

However, people need to understand the risks and negative consequences of manipulation and be able to recognize and resist these behaviors. This book will provide a comprehensive guide to these topics by examining dark psychology and manipulation techniques, explaining the negative impacts on mental health and interpersonal relationships, and offering practical guidance for preventing and defending against manipulation.

Dark psychology and manipulation are closely related concepts that deal with controlling and manipulating the emotional states and behaviors of others. Dark psychology uses subtle techniques to influence people's perceptions, emotions, and behaviors in order to gain a personal advantage or desired outcome. These techniques can be used in many situations, such as interpersonal relationships, work contexts, or even at the political level.

Emotional manipulation is one of the most common techniques used in dark psychology. It involves attempting to influence people's emotions in order to achieve a specific outcome. For example, a manipulator may use guilt or fear to convince someone to do something they otherwise would not do. This can negatively impact mental health and interpersonal relationships by creating a sense of insecurity and vulnerability in the victims of manipulation.

Manipulation can also occur in work contexts, where manipulators can use power and influence to gain a personal advantage or control the behavior of others. This can lead to a loss of trust and motivation in employees and a deterioration of work relationships.

Manipulation in the political arena is particularly concerning, as it can influence decisions made at the national level and affect people's lives. Political manipulation can occur through disseminating false information, using emotional persuasion techniques, or using power and influence to gain a personal or political advantage.

It is important to become aware of the techniques used and to recognize warning signs to prevent manipulation and protect oneself from negative consequences. It is also important to communicate assertively, set healthy boundaries, and recognize one's own values and needs. This book will provide a comprehensive guide to these topics, providing examples and practical strategies for preventing and resisting manipulation.

In summary, the introduction to dark psychology and manipulation is an important step in understanding these issues and defending oneself against these harmful behaviors in daily life. This book will provide a comprehensive and informative guide to these topics.

Definition of dark psychology and manipulation

Dark psychology is a term often used to describe a set of techniques and practices aimed at controlling and influencing others through the use of psychological methods. These methods may include emotional control, manipulation of perceptions and opinions, creation of dependency, and subtle persuasion. Dark psychology is often used by individuals seeking personal gain at the expense of others. It can significantly negatively affect the mental health and interpersonal relationships of manipulated individuals. Manipulation is an important aspect of dark psychology that focuses on the use of persuasion techniques and suggestibility to influence the decisions and actions of others. Manipulation can take many forms, from simple verbal persuasion to complex psychological strategies. Sometimes, manipulation can be difficult to recognize as seemingly positive motivations or friendly relationships may disguise it. However, it is important to be aware of the signs of manipulation and to protect oneself against these harmful behaviors.

Dark psychology and manipulation can be used in many different situations, including personal relationships, professional contexts, and politics. In interpersonal relationships, dark psychology and manipulation can be used to maintain unequal power or create emotional dependencies. For example, a manipulator may use emotional control to prevent a partner from making autonomous decisions or to make them feel guilty or inadequate. In the professional context, dark psychology and manipulation can be used to gain control over personnel decisions or influence colleagues' opinions and actions. In politics, manipulation is often used to influence public opinion or gain an advantage over opponents.

It is important to be aware of the techniques used and be able to recognize them to prevent the negative effects of dark psychology and manipulation. For example, it is important to be able to identify emotional control, such as blame-shifting or minimizing, and know how to resist these methods. Developing a strong sense of self-esteem and self-aware-ness is also important, as this can help resist manipulation techniques and maintain a balanced perspective.

It is important to recognize the signs of a manipulator and set boundaries for their actions. This may mean setting healthy boundaries and clearly communicating one's needs and desires. It is also important to seek support from reliable sources such as friends, family, or therapists if one suspects they are a victim of manipulation.

Developing assertive communication skills to manage manipulation situations effectively is also important. Assertive communication involves expressing one's thoughts and feelings clearly and respectfully without losing control or giving in to manipulation techniques. It is also important to have a good understanding of one's values and goals in life. This helps maintain a balanced perspective and not be influenced by people who use dark psychology or manipulation.

In conclusion, dark psychology and manipulation are harmful practices that can significantly negatively affect mental health and interpersonal relationships. However, with appropriate knowledge and awareness, people can protect themselves against these behaviors and prevent negative effects.

Exploration of the reasons why understanding these topics is important

Understanding dark psychology and manipulation is important for many reasons, both on a personal and societal level. On a personal level, knowledge of these topics can help protect oneself from toxic and manipulative relationships. Manipulation can significantly negatively impact mental health and emotional well-being and impair the ability to make autonomous decisions and keep healthy relationships. Through knowledge and understanding of dark psychology and manipulation, one can develop a higher sense of self-worth and self-awareness, which in turn can help protect against these harmful behaviors.

Understanding dark psychology and manipulation is important on a societal level because these behaviors are widespread and can affect many areas of society. For example, manipulation can be used in work contexts to gain power and control over employee decisions. It can also influence public opinion through the manipulation of media and mass communication channels.

In addition, understanding dark psychology and manipulation is important for preventing the spread of conspiracy theories and information manipulation. Nowadays, due to access to a large amount of online information, it is easy for people to fall victim to misinformation and information manipulation. By understanding the manipulation methods and techniques used to influence opinions and decisions, people can develop a higher level of critical thinking and the ability to analyze information in a more balanced and objective way.

Moreover, understanding dark psychology and manipulation is important for promoting healthy and positive relationships. On a personal level, understanding dark psychology and manipulation can help avoid toxic and harmful relationships. Knowing the signs and techniques of manipulation can help identify harmful or manipulative relationships and build healthier and more positive relationships based on transparency, trust, and reciprocity.

Understanding dark psychology and manipulation is important to a more balanced and happier life. When you understand the methods used to influence the decisions and opinions of others, you become less vulnerable to these behaviors and develop a greater ability to recognize and resist these negative behaviors.

For example, if you know the manipulation techniques used to control others, you can recognize these behaviors and take appropriate measures to protect yourself and your relationships. This can include setting clear boundaries and limitations, learning effective communication skills, and building relationships based on trust and transparency.

Understanding dark psychology and manipulation is important on a societal level because these behaviors can affect many areas of society. For example, manipulation can be used in work contexts to gain power and control over personnel decisions and can also influence public opinion through the manipulation of media and mass communication. Understanding these behaviors can help recognize and resist these negative behaviors and can also help promote a more equitable and balanced culture where relationships are based on transparency, trust, and reciprocity.

In addition, understanding dark psychology and manipulation is important to prevent the spread of conspiracy theories and information manipulation. With access to a large amount of online information, it is easy for people to fall victim to misinformation and information manipulation. By understanding the manipulation methods and techniques used to influence opinions and decisions, it is possible to develop greater critical thinking and the ability to analyze information in a more balanced and objective way. This can help prevent and resist these manipulations and promote a culture based on transparency, integrity, and responsibility. Additionally, understanding dark psychology and manipulation can help prevent the spread of misinformation and conspiracy theories and develop greater critical thinking and the ability to analyze information in a balanced and objective way. Ultimately, understanding dark psychology and manipulation is an important step towards a more balanced and happier life, both personally and socially.

Being aware of the manipulation methods and techniques used to influence the decisions and opinions of others can help to recognize and resist these negative behaviors, as well as develop healthy and positive relationships based on transparency, trust, and reciprocity.

Examination of information sources and techniques used to conduct research in this field

Examining the sources of information and techniques used to conduct research in the field of "dark psychology" and manipulation can be very complex due to the controversial nature of this topic. Dark psychology and manipulation are often described as negative techniques that aim to influence the perception and behavior of people.

In general, the sources of information used for research in this field include books, scientific articles, expert interviews, and online sources. However, it is important to note that many of these materials may be subject to distortions or a partial representation of facts, so verifying their reliability and credibility is important.

Regarding the techniques used for research, these may vary depending on the specific focus of the study. For example, some research may use quantitative research methods such as surveys or questionnaires to collect data, while others may be based on behavioral observations or qualitative interviews. In both cases, it is important to use a rigorous scientific approach and apply quality control practices to ensure the validity and reliability of the results.

It is also important to consider the ethical context when conducting research in this field. For example, it would be inappropriate to use dark psychology techniques or manipulation on individuals without their consent or for purposes that may cause them harm or stress.

In general, it is crucial to be extremely cautious in approaching this topic and rely on reliable sources and rigorous research techniques to conduct valid and reliable research. It is also important to respect ethical principles and not apply dark psychology and manipulation techniques for negative or harmful purposes. Understanding this topic requires a critical approach and careful evaluation of information sources and research techniques.

2

Human nature and manipulation

Human nature and manipulation are very complex and controversial topics. On one hand, human nature is constantly evolving and can be influenced by many factors, including culture, education, life experiences, and individual personality. On the other hand, manipulation is a technique used to influence the thinking and behavior of people, often with negative intentions. Human nature is a very extensive topic that covers many areas, including psychology, philosophy, anthropology, and sociology. Human nature has been studied for centuries by many cultures and disciplines, but there is still no definitive explanation for what makes humans unique compared to other animals. Many theories attempt to explain human nature, including the theory of evolution, Freud's theory of personality, and Jung's theory of personality.

Manipulation, on the other hand, is a technique used to influence the thinking and behavior of people. Manipulation can take many forms, such as persuasion, suggestibility, and hypnosis. Manipulation can be used for both positive and negative purposes. It can, for example, be used to help people overcome their fears or change their negative habits, but it can also be used to influence people's decisions or exploit their weaknesses. Human nature and manipulation are two very different aspects of human psychology, but they can also be closely related. Human nature can influence a person's propensity to be manipulated, and manipulation can influence a person's human nature. For example, a person who is manipulable due to their lack of self-esteem or a vulnerable personality can be induced to change their perception of themselves and the world around them.

In general, understanding human nature and manipulation is important for many disciplines, including psychology, sociology, and criminology. Knowledge of human nature and its influencing factors can help to understand human behavior and predict how people might react in specific situations. This knowledge can also be used to help people improve themselves and overcome their limitations. On the other hand, understanding manipulation is important for preventing its negative use and defending oneself from those who use it for harmful purposes. Furthermore, human nature and manipulation are also important for understanding the mechanisms that guide society and culture and education's influence on shaping human personality. Culture and education can influence a person's human nature, making them more open and accepting or more closed and intolerant. Manipulation, on the other hand, can be used to influence culture and education, ensuring that people adopt specific opinions and behaviors. In conclusion, human nature and manipulation are two very important aspects of human psychology that deserve further study and research. Their understanding can help to understand human behavior and prevent the negative use of manipulation. Additionally, understanding human nature and manipulation is important for shaping human personality and building a more just and inclusive society.

Analysis of how innate characteristics of human nature influence manipulation

The analysis of how innate characteristics of human nature influence manipulation is a topic of great importance in understanding how people can be influenced or controlled from the outside. Human nature consists of a set of traits, qualities, and abilities that are part of our existence and can influence our decisions and behaviors. These characteristics can be innate or acquired through experience and can have significant impacts on an individual's manipulability.

One of the most important innate characteristics that affect manipulation is personality. Personality is a set of distinctive traits that describe how a person thinks, behaves, and relates to others. Some people have a more open and accommodating personality, while others are more reserved and harder to influence. Personality can impact a person's ability to resist external pressures and manipulative influences.

Another characteristic that affects manipulation is a tendency towards anxiety and panic. People who are more prone to anxiety are more easily influenced by emotions and fears and are, therefore, more vulnerable to manipulative messages that exploit these emotional states. These people are also more likely to react impulsively and without thinking through consequences, which can make them easier to manipulate.

Trust and self-esteem are two other characteristics that can significantly influence a person's manipulability. People with low self-esteem are more vulnerable to messages that suggest they are incapable or unworthy. Therefore, they are more susceptible to influences from people who offer them help or support. On the other hand, people with high self-esteem are less susceptible to manipulative influences, as they are more confident in their abilities and competencies.

Empathy and the ability to understand the feelings of others are additional innate characteristics that can influence a person's manipulability. More empathetic people are more sensitive to the emotions of others and, therefore, more likely to be influenced by those who appear sincere and genuine. However, this same ability for empathy can also make a person more resistant to manipulative influences, as they are able to recognize when someone is trying to influence their feelings or behavior.

Curiosity and openness to learning are other innate characteristics that can influence a person's manipulability. Curious and open learners tend to seek out information and critically evaluate sources, which can make it more difficult for manipulators to influence them. However, this same curiosity and openness to learning can also make a person more vulnerable to manipulative messages if they are not able to recognize trustworthy and reliable sources of information.

Finally, the ability to think critically and make reasoned decisions is another characteristic that influences a person's manipulability. People who can think critically and make decisions based on facts and reasoning are less susceptible to manipulative influences, as they can critically evaluate information and make decisions based on their values and beliefs.

In conclusion, the innate characteristics of human nature have a great influence on a person's manipulability. Personality, a propensity to anxiety and panic, confidence and self-esteem, empathy, curiosity and openness to learning, and the ability to think critically are all characteristics that can influence a person's decisions and behavior, making them more or less vulnerable to manipulative influences. It is important to understand these characteristics to recognize and resist manipulative influences and make informed decisions based on one's own values and beliefs.

However, this ability can also be subject to external influences, such as misinformation or false information, if one does not pay attention to verifying sources and the validity of the information. In summary, innate characteristics of human nature can significantly influence a person's manipulability, and understanding and consciously using them can help protect oneself and others from manipulative influences. It is important to be aware of one's weaknesses and how they can be exploited by those attempting to manipulate and to develop strategies to protect oneself and resist manipulative influences by relying on reason and facts rather than emotions or external influences.

On the other hand, people who tend to react impulsively or base their decisions on emotions are more vulnerable to manipulative influences. In summary, many innate characteristics of human nature, such as personality, propensity for anxiety, confidence and self-esteem, empathy, curiosity, and ability to think critically and make rational decisions, can influence an individual's manipulability. However, it is important to note that no single characteristic definitively determines an individual's manipulability and that many other factors, such as education, experience, and specific circumstances, can influence a person's manipulability.

Exploration of the motivations that drive people to manipulate others

Manipulation is a behavior used by many people to influence or control the actions and decisions of others. This behavior can be motivated by a variety of factors, including a lack of control, fear, selfishness, the need for power, and a lack of empathy.

One of the most common reasons people manipulate others is a lack of control. Many people need to feel like they have control over situations and people around them, and manipulation provides a way for them to gain that control. For example, a person who feels insecure about their job might try to manipulate their boss or colleagues to secure a safer position or a salary increase.

Fear is another factor that drives people to manipulate others. Fear can come from a variety of sources, including the fear of being hurt, being judged, or losing something important. For example, a person who is afraid of being fired might manipulate their colleagues to secure a safer position at work.

Selfishness is another reason why people manipulate others. Selfish people are primarily focused on their own needs and desires and are willing to do anything to get what they want, even if it means manipulating others. For example, selfish people might manipulate their family or friends to get what they want.

The need for power is another factor that drives people to manipulate others. People who are obsessed with power are often willing to do anything to gain power and control over situations and people around them. For example, a politician who is obsessed with power may manipulate their voters or party members to gain power and control.

Finally, the lack of empathy is a factor that drives many people to manipulate others. People who lack empathy cannot put themselves in the shoes of others and understand their experiences and perspectives. This can make it easier for them to manipulate others, as they are not able to understand or consider the consequences of their actions on others. For example, a person without empathy may manipulate friends or family members to get what they want without considering the negative effects this may have on them.

It is important to note that manipulation can be harmful to both those who experience it and those who engage in it. Relationships based on manipulation are often destructive and can cause long-term damage to the self-esteem, trust, and emotional health of the individuals involved.

It is important to be aware of the signs of manipulation and know how to recognize them to avoid manipulation and protect oneself and others. Here are some of the most common signs of manipulation:

1. Ambiguous language: People who manipulate often use ambiguous language to confuse others and make it harder for them to understand what is really going on.
2. Exploiting emotions: People who manipulate often exploit the emotions of others to get what they want. They may use guilt or fear, for example, to influence the decisions of others.
3. Putting others in competition: People who manipulate often put others in a competition to create division and destabilize their position.
4. Giving false hope: People who manipulate often give false hope to get others to do what they want.
5. Playing on pity: People who manipulate often appeal to the pity of others to get their help.
6. Playing the victim: People who manipulate often play the victim to get attention and empathy from others.

It is important to recognize these signs and take measures to protect oneself and others to protect oneself from manipulation. Here are some tips to prevent manipulation:

1. Build self-esteem: Manipulation is easier when people have low self-esteem. Developing self-esteem and confidence can help protect oneself from manipulation.
2. Learn to say "no": Knowing how to say "no" and standing by one's principles can help protect oneself from manipulation.
3. Set clear boundaries: Setting clear boundaries and defending one's limits can help protect oneself from manipulation.
4. Learn to recognize one's emotions: Learning to recognize and manage one's emotions can help protect oneself from manipulation.
5. Seek support: Seeking support from friends, family, or professionals can help protect oneself from manipulation and manage difficult situations.
6. Learn to communicate assertively: Assertive communication can help protect oneself from manipulation by allowing one to express their thoughts and feelings clearly and decisively.
7. Be suspicious of offers that sound too good to be true: If something sounds too good to be true, it probably is. Being suspicious of offers that seem too good to be true can help protect oneself from manipulation. In general, it is important to be aware of the signs of manipulation and take steps to protect oneself and others from this negative behavior.
8. Be aware of one's vulnerabilities: Knowing one's vulnerabilities and weak points can help protect oneself from manipulation.

It is important to be aware of these signs and have a strong sense of self-worth and good communication skills to protect oneself from manipulation. A communication skill called "assertive communication" involves the clear and direct expression of opinions, desires, and needs without compromising the rights of others. It is also important to recognize one's own values and needs and make decisions based on these values rather than being influenced by the manipulation of others. In extreme cases, ending the relationship with a manipulator may be necessary to preserve one's emotional health and integrity.

Analysis of the personalities and common personality traits of manipulators

The analysis of manipulators' personalities and common personality traits is a topic of significant interest in psychology, as manipulation can negatively impact people's lives and their interpersonal relationships. Although there is no specific psychological profile of manipulators, some personality traits are often associated with this behavior. These traits include:

1. Narcissism: Manipulators often have a strong need to feel superior and control over others, which can manifest in excessive self-confidence and a lack of empathy for others.
2. Psychopathology: Some manipulators may suffer from mental disorders such as antisocial personality or psychopathy. These disorders can impair their ability to build healthy relationships and respect others' boundaries.
3. Power-seeking: Manipulation is often motivated by the need to gain and maintain power and control over others, which can manifest in the constant pursuit of advantage over others and a lack of scruples in pursuing their own goals.
4. Insecure emotions: Manipulators can be insecure about their own emotions and interpersonal relationships. This insecurity can lead them to control others' emotions to feel more secure and in control.
5. Emotional intelligence: Manipulators often have a good understanding of other's emotions and know how to use them to their advantage. This can be demonstrated in their ability to read nonverbal signals and understand others' motivations.
6. Lack of empathy: Manipulators often have little empathy for others and are insensitive to their needs and feelings. This can lead them to be indifferent to the negative impact of their manipulation on others.
7. Machiavellian behavior: Manipulators may tend to use Machiavellian techniques to achieve their goals. This behavior can manifest in lies, deception, tricks, and other dishonest behaviors to gain control or advantage over others.

In general, manipulators often have high self-esteem and low empathy for others. This can lead them to use control and persuasion techniques to gain power and control over others. However, it is important to note that not all people with these traits are manipulators and that manipulation is not always negative. In many cases, manipulation can be used to achieve positive goals and influence others constructively.

Manipulators are often skilled at hiding their intentions and masking manipulative behavior. They can present themselves as friendly and accommodating people but use these techniques to gain control.

In many situations, manipulators can use fear, guilt, and deception to get their way. For example, they can threaten to end a relationship or make confidential information public to get what they want. They can also appeal to the emotions and fears of others to get them to do what they want.

Manipulators often also have a poor ability to take responsibility for their behavior and actions. Instead, they tend to blame others and minimize the consequences of their actions.

It's important to be able to recognize manipulative behavior and protect oneself in such situations. This includes recognizing signals of dishonest persuasion techniques and setting clear boundaries to protect oneself.

It's also important to work on one's self-esteem and ability to communicate assertively. This can help reduce vulnerability to manipulation and maintain a healthy and balanced relationship with others.

In some cases, manipulators can also benefit from therapies such as psychotherapy or behavioral therapy. These therapies can help treat underlying personality disorders that contribute to manipulative behavior and learn new, healthier, and more constructive patterns of behavior.

In summary, analyzing the common personality traits of manipulators can help understand manipulative behavior and prevent its negative consequences. Manipulation can have a negative impact on people's lives and their interpersonal relationships. Some common personality traits of manipulators include narcissism, power-hunger, lack of empathy, and

Machiavellian behavior. However, it is important to note that not all people who exhibit these traits are manipulators and that manipulation is not always negative. Manipulators can be very skillful at hiding their intentions and using different techniques such as fear, guilt, and deception to get their way. It is important to be aware of manipulation signals and learn how to protect oneself and one's interests in manipulative situations.

3

Common manipulation techniques

Many manipulation techniques can be used to influence others and gain control. Here are some of the most common techniques:

1. Gaslighting: Manipulating the perception of others to make them uncertain about reality. For example, a manipulator may deny saying or doing something they actually said or did.
2. Triangulation: Manipulating relationships between different people to gain control or advantage. For example, a manipulator may create tensions between two people to get their way.
3. Fear, guilt, and shame: Manipulating the emotions of others to make them do what they want. For example, a manipulator may appeal to the fear, guilt, or shame of others to make them do what they want.
4. Flattery and praise: Manipulating the perception of others through praise and flattery. For example, a manipulator may flatter someone to get their help or support.
5. Threats: Manipulating the perception of others through threats. For example, a manipulator may threaten to end a relationship or disclose confidential information to get what they want.

6. Deceptive persuasion: Manipulating others through the use of deceptive persuasion techniques. For example, a manipulator may use reality distortion or falsification of information to induce others to do what they want.
7. Exploitation: Manipulating others through the use of exploitation techniques. For example, a manipulator may exploit the vulnerability or dependence of others to get what they want.

In general, it is important to be aware of manipulation techniques and their negative consequences and to learn to recognize and protect oneself from these behaviors.

Gaslighting is a particularly dangerous manipulation technique that involves manipulating others' perceptions of reality. The manipulator denies having said or done something and constantly challenges the memory and perception of others, creating confusion and uncertainty. This behavior can negatively impact victims' self-confidence and interpersonal relationships and cause stress, anxiety, and depression.

Triangulation is a manipulation technique that involves creating tensions between different people to gain control or advantage. The manipulator may do this by involving third parties in the situation, creating rivalries, and destroying trust between the people involved. This can be particularly destructive for interpersonal relationships and can create divisions and conflicts.

The use of fear, guilt, and shame is a manipulation technique that involves using negative emotions to induce victims to do what the manipulator wants. The manipulator can exploit these emotions by appealing to fear of negative consequences, guilt for causing problems, or shame for making mistakes. This can negatively impact victims' emotional well-being and lead them to take actions that go against their interests or values.

Flattery and flattering are manipulation techniques that involve the use of positive and flattering words to influence others. The manipulator may use these techniques to obtain support or help from victims, but this can also lead them to perform actions that go against their interests or values. Flattery and flattering can also negatively affect the victims' self-confidence and judgment and lead to deeper and more harmful manipulation.

Threats are a manipulation technique that involves the threat of negative consequences to induce victims to do what the manipulator wants. The manipulator may threaten to end a relationship, disclose confidential information, or cause physical or emotional harm to get their way. This can cause the victim to develop fear and dependence on the manipulator and negatively affect their emotional well-being.

Deceptive persuasion is a manipulation technique involving deceptive persuasion techniques, such as distorting reality or falsifying information, to induce victims to do what the manipulator wants. This can cause the victim to perform actions against their interests or believe in false information.

The use of exploitation techniques is a manipulation technique that involves exploiting the vulnerability or dependence of victims to get one's way. The manipulator can exploit the weaknesses or fears of the victims to obtain their help or support or to gain control over their lives. This can negatively affect the emotional and physical well-being of the victims and cause them to perform actions that go against their values or interests.

In general, it is important to be aware of manipulation techniques and their negative effects and to learn to recognize and protect oneself from these behaviors. Open communication, understanding of one's emotions, and building healthy relationships can help prevent manipulation and protect emotional and physical well-being.

Speech about the most common manipulation techniques

Manipulation is a dark art that some people use to get what they want from others without them noticing or being able to resist. There are many manipulation techniques, some of which are very common and used daily. These techniques often rely on the use of psychological and persuasion techniques. They are designed to make the manipulated person feel that their decision is their own and not influenced by the person manipulating them.

Emotional control is one of the most common manipulation techniques. This technique is based on the fact that emotions are very powerful and can influence people's decisions. The manipulator uses this fact to their advantage, trying to evoke negative or positive emotions in a person to make them feel a certain way and get what they want. For example, a manipulator may use fear or shame to make a person feel guilty and get what they want from them.

Verbal manipulation is another very common manipulation technique. This technique is based on words and how they are used. A verbal manipulator uses words to make the manipulated person feel that they are doing the right thing, even if they actually do the opposite. For example, a verbal manipulator may use phrases like "trust me," "don't worry, everything will be fine," or "it's the only right thing to do" to make the manipulated person believe that they are doing the right thing, even if they are not.

Information control is another very common manipulation technique. This technique is based on the fact that people make decisions based on what they know or believe they know. A manipulator who controls information can hide or distort information to make the manipulated person make the decision he wants. For example, a manipulator could hide important information or distort facts to make someone believe that a product is better than it actually is.

There are many other manipulation techniques, but these are the most common ones. It's important to note that these techniques are designed to be subtle and not recognized by the manipulated person. This makes manipulation dangerous because the person being subjected to it may not be able to recognize that it's happening and, therefore, won't be able to resist it. It's important to be aware of these techniques and learn to recognize them when they're being used to protect oneself from manipulation. This can be done by learning to understand one's own feelings and emotions and recognizing when they're being used to influence one's decisions.

Additionally, it's important to learn to ask questions and seek different sources to verify if the information being received is complete and accurate. Finally, it's important to learn to say no to requests that don't feel right or seem out of place. This can be difficult, especially when being manipulated by someone known and trusted, but it's important to learn to set boundaries and protect oneself. In summary, manipulation is a dark art used by some people to get what they want from others. It's important to be aware of the most common manipulation techniques, such as emotional control, verbal manipulation, and information control, and learn to protect oneself from them. Only then can one make informed and autonomous decisions and not become a victim of manipulation.

Analysis of the way these techniques are used and their effects on people

The manipulation techniques described above are used in many different situations, from personal relationships to work and political contexts. These techniques can strongly impact people and impair their ability to make autonomous and informed decisions.

Emotional control is a technique that relies on the power of emotions to influence people's decisions. This technique can be very powerful, as emotions can have a significant impact on how we think and act. For example, if someone makes us feel guilty, we may be more likely to do something to alleviate that feeling, even if we don't actually want to. Emotional control can be particularly dangerous when used by people who have some power or influence over us, such as a spouse or employer.

Verbal manipulation is a technique that relies on the power of words to influence people's decisions. This technique can be very subtle, as words can be used to make people believe they are doing the right thing, even if they are not. For example, a verbal manipulator may use comforting or reassuring phrases to make the manipulated person feel like they are making the right decision, even if they are actually doing the opposite. This technique can be particularly dangerous when used by people who hold an authoritative position or influence, such as a political leader or business representative.

Information control is a technique that relies on the power of information to influence people's decisions. This technique can be very subtle, as information can be manipulated or hidden to influence people's perceptions of a particular situation or product. For example, a manipulative information controller might hide important facts or distort reality to make people believe that a product is better than it really is. This technique can be particularly dangerous when used by companies or organizations that have an interest in selling a product or promoting a specific ideology.

Furthermore, these manipulation techniques can have negative effects on people's mental health. Manipulation can cause stress, anxiety, depression, and psychological disorders like post-traumatic stress disorder. The lack of autonomy and control over one's own life can also lead to a sense of despair and helplessness.

It is important to be aware of the techniques that can be used against us and learn to recognize them to avoid manipulation. It is also important to develop a strong sense of self-esteem and a solid support network so that we can face situations of manipulation with greater security and confidence. Additionally, it is important to learn to communicate assertively and to say "no" when we feel uncomfortable or pressured to do something we do not want to do.

In summary, manipulation techniques are used in many different situations and can strongly influence people and their decisions. It is important to be aware of the techniques used and to protect oneself and one's mental health to avoid manipulation.

Awareness, self-esteem, and assertive communication are all important tools to prevent manipulation and protect one's mental health. Having a support network of friends and family who support us and help us recognize and resist manipulation techniques is also important. Ultimately, it is important to be aware of manipulation techniques and learn how to protect one's integrity and autonomy to lead a happier and more fulfilling life.

Building self-esteem and a solid support network and learning assertive communication are also important. However, despite these efforts, it may still be difficult to completely escape manipulation, especially when it is exercised by individuals who hold significant power or influence over us. In any case, it is important to recognize the signs of manipulation and seek help if one feels victimized by these techniques.

It is important to be aware of one's vulnerability and how manipulation techniques can be used against us to prevent manipulation. It is also important to develop a good understanding of one's values and limits in order to make informed and autonomous decisions. Additionally, it is important to develop assertive communication skills and learn how to recognize and address manipulation situations when they arise. Finally, it is important to seek support from friends, family, or professionals if one feels victimized by manipulation or needs help processing emotions and thoughts associated with a manipulation situation. This support can be crucial in regaining self-confidence and regaining control of one's life.

In summary, manipulation techniques are a serious problem that can have a negative impact on people's lives. However, there are ways to avoid manipulation and protect oneself from the negative consequences it can cause. Learning to recognize and address manipulation situations and developing a good understanding of one's values and limits are important steps in preventing manipulation and maintaining control over one's life.

Exercise: Identifying Manipulation Techniques Used in Daily Life

There are many manipulation techniques used in daily life. Here are some of the most common:

1. Body language: People can manipulate others using body language to send subliminal messages or influence the emotions of others.
2. Evasive responses: People can avoid direct questions or provide misleading information to conceal the truth or deceive others.

3. Appeal to emotion: People can manipulate others using emotion to influence their perception or decision.
4. Wordplay: Words can be used in a manipulative way to influence the perception of things or to create confusion.
5. Threats or blackmail: People can manipulate others using threats or blackmail to get what they want.
6. Persuasion: People can manipulate others using persuasion or convincing to influence their opinion or decision.
7. False statements: People can manipulate others using false statements or inaccurate information to influence their perception or decision.
8. Use of gratification: People can manipulate others using gratification or reward to get them to do what they want.
9. Use of nostalgia: People can manipulate others using nostalgia or evoking positive memories to influence their opinion or decision.
10. Use of repetition: People can manipulate others by continuously repeating a message to influence their perception or decision.

These are just some examples of manipulation techniques used in daily life. It's important to be aware of these techniques and learn to recognize them to protect oneself from manipulation.

Situation	Manipulation technique	Experienced emotion	Possible way to deal with it in the future
I have decided to buy a product advertised as "the best on the market."	Appeal to authority	Deceived	Research the product and compare it with other manufacturers before purchasing it.
My employer asked me to work on the weekend because it's a 'career opportunity.	Threatened	Forced	Discuss the terms and conditions of the extra work with the employer and consider alternatives.
My friend asked me to lend him money because "it will make me feel like a good person.	Appeal to emotions	Exploited	Politely refuse or find alternatives to help my friend.

Exercise

Situation	Manipulation technique	Experienced emotion	Possible way to deal with it in the future

4

Recognizing manipulation

Manipulation is a behavior used to influence the thoughts, emotions, or behavior of another person for one's own benefit. It can be carried out by individuals, groups, or organizations and can have negative consequences for the manipulated person. Here are some ways to recognize manipulation:

1. Ambiguous communication: Manipulation often occurs when a person's words or actions are unclear or vague. This can create confusion and make it difficult to understand what is really going on.
2. Persistent beliefs: Manipulation often involves persistent or repetitive beliefs by the manipulator. This can be done by repeating a message or through constant pressure to persuade the other person.
3. Appeal to emotions: Manipulation often involves an appeal to emotions such as fear or excitement. This can be done through the use of images or emotional stories that influence the other person's emotions.
4. Threats or blackmail: Manipulation often involves threats or blackmail to get what one wants. This can be done through the

threat of negative consequences if the other person does not act as requested.

5. Forced conviction: Manipulation often involves a forced conviction, in which the manipulator uses persuasion or pressure to influence the other person's decision.
6. Use of authority or position: Manipulation often involves the use of authority or power to influence the decisions or actions of another person.
7. False statements or misinformation: Manipulation often involves the use of false statements or misinformation to influence the perception or decisions of another person.

It is important to become aware of these signals and learn to recognize them to protect oneself from manipulation. It is also important to be able to communicate clearly and directly and not be intimidated by pressure or the persistent beliefs of other people.

Furthermore, it is important to be able to evaluate information and consider sources before deciding or taking a stance. It is important to be aware of one's well-being and how decisions can impact one's life.

It is also important to be able to communicate assertively and refuse to be manipulated. This means expressing one's thoughts and feelings directly and clearly, without giving in to the pressure or manipulation of other people.

In many cases, manipulation is perpetrated by individuals who are trying to gain control over others or get what they want to their advantage. This can happen in many contexts, such as in family, the workplace, romantic relationships, or friendships.

Recognizing warning signs and developing a strong sense of self-worth and self-awareness are important to protect oneself from manipulation. This means being aware of one's own emotions and thoughts and knowing what is important to us and what is not.

Furthermore, it is important to manage one's own emotions effectively and not react impulsively to manipulation situations. This can be done through practices such as mindfulness or meditation, which help us stay calm and react rationally to difficult situations.

Finally, it is important to surround oneself with positive and supportive people who encourage us to be ourselves and not give in to manipulation. This can be achieved through creating healthy and positive relationships with friends, family, and colleagues who support and encourage us to be strong and resist manipulation.

Speech about difficulties in identifying manipulation

Manipulation is a difficult-to-identify phenomenon that poses a threat to democracy and society. Manipulation can be carried out through various means, such as disseminating fake news, creating artificial public opinions, and distorting facts. However, it is possible to identify manipulation by following some simple steps.

Firstly, it is important to be able to identify reliable sources of information. This means checking the credibility of sources, their method of information gathering, and their objectivity. This way, one can avoid being influenced by fake or distorted news.

Secondly, paying attention to the language used in messages and content is important. Manipulation often hides behind words that evoke emotions or have been chosen to influence the perception of reality. For example, emotional or hyperbolic language may be used to create a distorted picture of reality.

Thirdly, it is important to recognize the manipulation of images and videos. This type of manipulation is particularly difficult to identify, as it is often used to create a false or distorted image of reality. For example, the software can be used to modify images or videos to make them look different from what they really are.

Finally, it is important to be aware of the manipulation techniques used by the media and those in power. These techniques may include the spread of fake news, the creation of artificial public opinions, and the distortion of facts. Understanding these techniques will help to recognize manipulation and protect the ability to make informed decisions.

In conclusion, manipulation is a difficult-to-identify phenomenon, but it is possible to avoid being influenced by it by following some simple steps. It is important to pay attention to reliable sources of information, the language used in messages, the manipulation of images and videos, and manipulation techniques.

However, it is important to emphasize that manipulation is not just a problem for individuals but for society as a whole. Manipulation can create social divisions and conflicts, influence political decisions, and distort reality perception. It is crucial for society to develop a culture of critical information gathering and source verification to combat manipulation. This requires appropriate education for individuals and greater awareness of the mechanisms of manipulation.

Additionally, the media must take on their role as guardians and be transparent and objective in their reporting. Furthermore, authorities should work to protect democracy and society from manipulation. This can be achieved through media regulation and punishment for those responsible for manipulation. However, it is important that such regulation does not restrict freedom of expression and the press.

Furthermore, emerging technologies such as artificial intelligence and blockchain can be used to combat manipulation. For example, artificial intelligence can be used to detect false news or manipulated content, while blockchain can be used to ensure transparency and immutability of data.

In summary, manipulation is a complex and constantly evolving problem, but it can be avoided through a culture of critical information gathering, appropriate education, responsible regulation, and the use of emerging technologies. The fight against manipulation is crucial for society's stability and security and for preserving freedom and democracy.

Tips for recognizing warning signs of manipulation

There are some common warning signs that may indicate manipulation by someone:

1. Persistent behavior: If someone persistently and stubbornly tries to convince you, it may be a signal of manipulation.
2. False emotions: If someone seems emotionally false to you or if their emotions seem out of place, it may be a signal of manipulation.
3. Implicit threats: If someone makes you feel guilty or threatens you implicitly, it may be a signal of manipulation.
4. Confusion: If you feel confused or unsure about your decisions, it may be a signal of manipulation.
5. Isolation: If someone tries to isolate you from others or limit your interaction with others, it may signal manipulation.
6. Vague speech: If someone speaks in a vague or evasive way, it may be a signal of manipulation.
7. Inconsistent behavior: If someone acts inconsistently or unreliably, it may be a signal of manipulation.

Recognizing these warning signs is just the first step in protecting oneself from manipulation. It is also important to learn to say no, set boundaries and develop a strong sense of self-worth and solid self-awareness. Certainly, recognizing warning signs is important to protect oneself from manipulation, but it is only part of the puzzle. Defending oneself against manipulation also requires a strong sense of self-worth and a good understanding of oneself and one's values.

In addition, it is important to learn assertive communication, which means expressing one's thoughts and feelings clearly and respectfully without allowing anyone else to influence one's decisions or behaviors. It is also helpful to recognize and manage one's emotions to avoid being influenced by emotional threats or blackmail.

Furthermore, it is important to understand that manipulation is not always easy to recognize and often can be hidden behind seemingly innocent or even positive behaviors. For example, a manipulator may pretend to be concerned about your well-being or share your opinion only to get what they want. It is important to question the thoughts and actions of others and evaluate their integrity to defend oneself against manipulation. Asking whether their intentions are truly sincere or if there is a hidden motive behind their action can help identify manipulation.

Exercise: Evaluating situations to identify manipulation

Here's an example of how you could evaluate a situation to identify manipulation:

Suppose a friend has invited you to an event to present their new product. When you arrive at the event, you realize that your friend has asked you to buy the product, even if you're not interested or don't need it. To evaluate the situation and identify manipulation, you could ask yourself:

1. Is my friend insistent on me buying the product? Yes, he seems very insistent and doesn't respect my decision of not being interested.
2. Does my friend seem emotionally fake, or are his emotions out of place? No, he seems emotionally involved in the product presentation.
3. Is my friend making me feel guilty or implicitly threatening me? No, he's not making me feel guilty or threatening me, but his persistence makes me uncomfortable.
4. Do I feel confused or unsure about my decisions? Yes, I feel confused and don't know how to handle the situation with my friend.
5. Is my friend trying to isolate me from others or limit my interaction with other people? No, he's not trying to isolate me from others or limit my interaction with other people.
6. Is my friend speaking in a vague or evasive way? No, my friend is very precise in the product presentation.
7. Is my friend acting in an inconsistent or unreliable way? No, my friend seems consistent and reliable in his actions.

Here is a table summarizing the evaluation of the situation:

Question	Answer
Is my friend insistent on me purchasing the product?	Yes
Does my friend seem emotionally insincere or out of place?	No
Does my friend make me feel guilty or implicitly threaten me?	No
Do I feel confused or unsure of my decisions?	Yes
Is my friend trying to isolate me from others or limit my interaction with other people?	No
Is my friend speaking in a vague or evasive manner?	No
Is my friend acting in an inconsistent or unreliable manner?	No

After answering these questions, you might conclude that your friend is trying to manipulate you because they are insistent on you purchasing the product even if you're not interested. They make you feel confused and uncomfortable with their insistence. In this case, you might want to set boundaries in your interaction with them and address the situation assertively to protect yourself from manipulation.

Based on this table, it can be inferred that your friend is trying to manipulate you because they are insistent on you purchasing the product, and they make you feel confused and uncomfortable with their insistence.

Here's an example of evaluating a situation to identify manipulation:

Red flag	Presence in the situation
Insistent behavior	Yes
False emotions	No
Implicit threats	Yes
Confusion	Yes
Isolation	No
Vague speech	Yes
Inconsistent behavior	No

In this example, there are warning signs of persistent behavior, implicit threats, confusion, and vague statements in the situation, which could suggest that manipulation is taking place. However, this is not definitive proof, and further evaluation or investigation may be necessary to determine if there is actually manipulation.

It is important to note that the presence of one or more warning signs does not necessarily mean that there is manipulation, but only that there is a possibility and further evaluation is required. Additionally, manipulation can take many forms, and not all warning signs will be present in every situation.

Exercise

Question	Answer

Red flag	Presence in the situation

5

Manipulation in interpersonal relationships

Manipulation is a common behavior in interpersonal relationships, where one person tries to influence another person's thoughts, feelings, or actions to satisfy their own needs or interests. Manipulation can be seen as a form of psychological influence that aims to influence the behavior of others without them realizing it.

In this chapter, we will explore the various types of manipulation, warning signs for identifying it, and strategies people can use to protect themselves. We will also examine how manipulation can affect interpersonal relationships and discuss how this behavior can be treated and managed.

Types of manipulation

There are many forms of manipulation, but some of the most common are emotional, psychological, physical, and verbal. Emotional manipulation involves using emotions to influence the decisions of others. Psychological manipulation involves the use of mental tricks to influence the thoughts and emotions of others. Physical manipulation involves the use of physical force to influence the behavior of others, while verbal manipulation involves the use of words to influence the thoughts and emotions of others.

Warning signs

There are many warning signs that can indicate the presence of manipulation in interpersonal relationships. These include persistent demands, not respecting others' decisions, a tendency to manipulate others' emotions, a tendency to make others feel guilty or implicitly threaten them, a tendency to confuse or make others uncertain, a tendency to isolate others from other people or restrict their interaction with others, a tendency to speak vaguely or evasively, and a tendency to act unreliably or inconsistently.

Self-protection strategies

Recognizing the warning signs and pursuing an assertive approach in interpersonal relationships is important to protect oneself from manipulation. An assertive approach involves the ability to express one's thoughts, emotions, and needs clearly and directly without being aggressive or submissive. It is also important to manage one's own emotions and not be influenced by others' emotions, especially when it comes to emotional manipulation.

Other self-protection strategies against manipulation include:

- Saying no and setting clear boundaries
- Having a strong sense of self-worth and self-efficacy
- Having a solid understanding of one's own values and needs
- Knowing one's own weaknesses and working to strengthen them
- Surrounding oneself with positive and reliable people
- Learning to seek support from friends, family, or professionals when needed

Impact on interpersonal relationships

Manipulation can have negative effects on interpersonal relationships, as it can create a destructive and dysfunctional dynamic. Manipulation can cause conflicts, tensions, and communication difficulties and can also lead to a loss of trust and respect toward the person who employs it. Furthermore, manipulation can cause the person who is being manipulated to lose their sense of self-worth and self-efficacy, as they may doubt their decisions and feel confused and uncertain.

Treatment and Management

It is important to identify the source of the behavior and understand its underlying causes to treat and manage manipulation in interpersonal relationships. In many cases, manipulation is the result of insecurities or deep fears, and understanding these can help find solutions that can meet the needs of both parties.

Additionally, it is important to work on one's self-esteem and self-efficacy, learn to manage emotions, and respond to manipulative behaviors in an assertive style. In cases of persistent or severe manipulation, seeking professional support from a therapist or counselor who can help manage the situation and find effective solutions may be helpful. Overall, manipulation is a common behavior in interpersonal relationships that can negatively impact individuals' psychological health and relationships. Learning to recognize manipulation signals and defend against them is important to avoid loss of self-esteem and maintain healthy and positive relationships.

Analysis of how manipulation is used in interpersonal relationships, such as in family, friendship, and romantic partnerships.

This section will explore how manipulation is used in interpersonal relationships such as family, friendship, and romantic relationships. First, let's talk about manipulation in the family. A family is a place where people often try to influence others to get what they want. For example, parents can emotionally control or emotionally blackmail their children into doing what they want. Parents can also use guilt or the threat of losing affection to get the desired behavior from their children. This type of manipulation can have a negative impact on the relationship between family members and the psychological well-being of the children.

Manipulation can also occur in friendships. Friends can use emotional control or emotional blackmail to influence each other. For example, a friend can threaten to end the friendship if the other person doesn't do what they want. This can lead to an unhealthy relationship and a loss of self-esteem for the manipulated person.

Finally, let's talk about manipulation in romantic relationships. Manipulation in romantic relationships can occur in many different ways. For example, a partner can use emotional control or emotional blackmail to influence the other. They can also use guilt or the threat of ending the relationship to get what they want. This type of manipulation can have a negative impact on the psychological well-being of the partners and the relationship itself.

Here is a detailed and extended example of how manipulation is used in family, friendships, and romantic relationships: In the family:

Suppose a parent wants their child to go to bed at 9 pm every night. Instead of politely and respectfully asking the child to go to bed, the parent may use manipulation to get what they want. For example, they may threaten to take away the privilege of watching TV if the child doesn't go to bed at 9 or blackmail the child by saying they won't love them anymore if they don't go to bed at that time. This type of manipulation can have a negative impact on the relationship between the parent and child, create tension, and cause the child to have lower self-esteem.

In friendships: Suppose two friends want to decide where to eat dinner together. One friend may use manipulation to get what they want, for example, by threatening to no longer be friends with the other if they don't go to the restaurant they want. This type of manipulation can lead to an unhealthy relationship and lower self-esteem for the manipulated friend.

In romantic relationships: Suppose a couple discusses where to spend their summer vacation. One partner may use manipulation to get what they want, for example, by threatening to end the relationship if they don't go to the place they want. This type of manipulation can have a negative impact on the partners' mental health and the relationship itself, causing tension and making it more difficult to find a solution that satisfies both.

In summary, these are just some examples of how manipulation is used in family, friendships, and romantic relationships. It is important to note that manipulation is not a healthy or acceptable behavior in any interpersonal relationship. We should always try to communicate openly and honestly, avoiding manipulation to get what we want.

It is important to engage in healthy relationships and communicate openly and honestly to avoid using manipulation as a means to get what you want. This way, you can build relationships based on mutual trust, respect, and understanding, which are essential for a happy and fulfilling life.

In summary, manipulation is a harmful behavior that can occur in many types of interpersonal relationships. Learning to recognize it, defend against it, and build healthy relationships is important for emotional well-being and the development of healthy and fulfilling relationships. Open and honest communication is crucial to building healthy relationships and avoiding manipulation. It is also important to recognize and defend against the signs of manipulation.

A speech about the negative impact that manipulation can have on these relationships

Manipulation can have significant negative consequences for interpersonal relationships. In a family, manipulation can undermine the trust and security of family members, create tensions and conflicts, and have a negative impact on the emotional health of family members.

For example, if a parent manipulates a child using emotional control or emotional blackmail, it can cause a reduction in the child's self-esteem and security. The child may feel overwhelmed and unable to make autonomous decisions, which can have long-lasting effects on their adult life. Manipulation by parents can also create an unhealthy relationship between family members, where there is no mutual respect or understanding.

Similarly, manipulation in friendships can destroy the trust and security that exists between friends. If one friend manipulates the other through emotional control or emotional blackmail, it can cause a reduction in the other friend's self-esteem and security. This can also cause tensions and conflicts in the relationship and ultimately destroy the relationship itself.

Manipulation in a relationship can also have significant negative effects on the relationship. For example, if one partner manipulates the other through emotional control or emotional blackmail, it can decrease the other partner's self-esteem and security. This can also create tensions and conflicts in the relationship and negatively impact the emotional health of the partners. Additionally, manipulation by a partner can create an unhealthy and dysfunctional relationship where there is no mutual respect or understanding.

Manipulation can also have negative effects on people's mental health and emotional safety. A person being repeatedly manipulated can lead to mental health problems such as anxiety, depression, and low self-esteem. These problems can have long-lasting effects on a person's life and negatively impact their ability to build healthy and fulfilling relationships.

In summary, it is important to be aware of the potential consequences of manipulation and take action to address it. This may include setting clear boundaries, learning effective communication skills, and seeking support from trusted friends, family, or a mental health professional if needed. It is also important to understand that the effects of manipulation can be long-lasting, and it takes time to heal and rebuild trust after experiencing manipulation.

However, with effort and support, it is possible to recover and build healthy relationships in the future. Finally, it is crucial to understand that all relationships should be based on mutual respect, trust, and understanding. Manipulation is a destructive force that can undermine these values and cause harm to people and relationships. By recognizing the signs of manipulation and acting, people can work to build healthy and fulfilling relationships with those around them.

Exercise: Identification and resolution of manipulation problems in interpersonal relationships

Identifying manipulation problems in interpersonal relationships is an important first step to resolving them and protecting emotional health and relationships. Here are some steps that can be helpful in identifying and resolving manipulation problems:

Recognize the signs of manipulation: It is important to be able to recognize the signs of manipulation, such as emotional control, emotional blackmail, false guilt, threat, and ambiguity.

Assess your situation: If you feel like you are a victim of manipulation, take time to assess your situation and understand how the manipulation is affecting your life and interpersonal relationships.

Set boundaries: Establishing healthy boundaries and communicating them clearly is important to protect yourself from manipulation. This can involve questioning manipulative behaviors and communicating your own needs and boundaries.

Communicate effectively: Learning clear and assertive communication can help prevent manipulation and deal with potentially manipulative situations.

Seek support: If manipulation is negatively impacting your life and interpersonal relationships, seeking support from trusted friends, family members, or a professional mental health expert can be helpful.

Work on your self-esteem: Manipulation can have a negative impact on people's self-esteem and sense of security. Therefore, working on your self-esteem and security can help protect you from manipulation and restore trust in relationships.

Evaluate the relationship: If manipulation occurs in a particular interpersonal relationship, it may be necessary to evaluate whether the relationship is healthy and whether it is possible to maintain it. In some cases, it may be necessary to make the decision to end the relationship to protect emotional health.

In summary, identifying and resolving manipulation problems in interpersonal relationships requires time, effort, and support.

Here is an example of a table for identifying and resolving manipulation problems in interpersonal relationships:

Steps	Details
Recognize signs of manipulation	- Develop awareness of common patterns of manipulation, such as emotional blackmail, lying, and control. - Take note of manipulative behaviors that occur in the relationship.
Evaluate one's involvement	- Reflect on whether one has been involved in manipulative behaviors. - Consider how one's lack of assertiveness or self-esteem may have been exploited.
Set clear boundaries	- Clearly communicate one's limits and expectations in the relationship. - Step back from situations that have been manipulated or have become too harmful.
Learn communication skills	- Learn to communicate assertively and manage conflicts constructively. - Develop the ability to listen and respect others' perspectives.
Seek support	- Seek help from friends, family, or a mental health professional if necessary. - Participate in support groups or therapy to help overcome the effects of manipulation.
Work on self-esteem	- Develop one's self-esteem and assertiveness. - Learn to say no and take care of oneself.
Build healthy relationships	- Develop relationships based on trust, respect, and mutual understanding. - Learn to identify and avoid manipulative behaviors in others.

This example table provides a structure for identifying and resolving manipulation problems in interpersonal relationships.

However, each situation is unique and may require a customized combination of these steps. The important thing is to take the time to recognize the signs of manipulation and take action to protect oneself and one's relationship.

Example of a Situation:

Steps to Overcoming Manipulation in Relationships	Description
Recognizing Signs of Manipulation	Becoming aware of common manipulation patterns and noting when they are being applied in the relationship.
Assessing Own Involvement	Recognizing involvement in manipulative behaviors and exploitation of one's own lack of assertiveness and self-esteem.
Setting Clear Boundaries	Communicating personal boundaries and expectations and withdrawing from manipulated or harmful situations.
Learning Communication Skills	Learning assertive communication, conflict resolution, listening, and respecting the perspectives of others.
Seeking Support	Seeking help from friends, family, or a professional mental health expert and participating in support groups or therapy.
Working on Self-Esteem	Developing self-worth and assertiveness, learning to say no, and self-care.
Building Healthy Relationships	Developing relationships based on trust, respect, and mutual understanding, identifying and avoiding manipulative behaviors.

Exercise

Steps	Details
Recognize signs of manipulation	
Evaluate one's involvement.	
Set clear boundaries	
Learn communication skills	
Seek support	
Work on self-esteem	
Build healthy relationships	

6

Manipulation in the workplace

Workplace manipulation can have negative effects on the mental health and careers of those involved. It can also impair productivity and collaboration within the team and worsen the work environment. Here are some of the most common types of workplace manipulation and how to deal with them.

1. Emotional blackmail. Emotional blackmail is a form of manipulation in which a person uses fear, guilt, or emotions to get what they want. This can happen in the workplace when a supervisor uses the threat of losing one's job. This can be very stressful and have negative impacts on the mental health of those involved.

How to deal with it: Talking to a supervisor or HR representative about inappropriate behavior is important. Additionally, one may consider seeking support from a counselor or attorney to protect their rights in the workplace.

2. Control. Control is a form of manipulation in which a person attempts to control the actions, decisions, or opinions of others. This can happen in the workplace when a supervisor tries to control the way an employee performs their work or attempts to influence their decisions. This can be very stressful and impair the employee's productivity.

How to deal with it: It is important to set clear boundaries with the supervisor and communicate expectations about how the work should be performed. Additionally, one may consider seeking support from a counselor or attorney to protect their rights in the workplace.

3. Misinformation. Misinformation is a form of manipulation where a person provides false or misleading information to influence the decisions of others. This can happen in the workplace when a supervisor provides false information about a project or employee to influence the decisions of others. This can be very stressful and can negatively impact productivity and team collaboration.

How to deal with it: It is important to seek reliable information from multiple sources before making important decisions. Additionally, it is important to speak with the supervisor and request clarification regarding the information provided to ensure accuracy. In some cases, it may be helpful to discuss the situation with a representative from the human resources department or an attorney to protect one's own interests and those of the team.

4. Poor communication. Poor communication can be considered a form of manipulation because it can prevent people from having complete and accurate information to make informed decisions. This can happen in the workplace when a supervisor fails to provide complete information or withholds important information.

How to deal with it: It is important to ask the supervisor for clarification and complete information and, if necessary, discuss the situation with a representative from the human resources department to ensure all information is available. Open and transparent communication is important to avoid manipulation and ensure a positive and productive work environment. Manipulation in the workplace can be challenging to deal with, but with the right strategy and support, it is possible to address and prevent it.

It is important to take these behaviors seriously and seek help, if necessary, to protect one's own mental health and career. With a little awareness and the willingness to act, creating a more positive and productive work environment for everyone is possible.

Analysis of how manipulation is used in the workplace

Let's examine in detail how manipulation is used in the workplace and how it can impact employees and team dynamics. Emotional blackmail is a common form of workplace manipulation. This method uses fear, guilt, or emotions to get what one wants. For example, a supervisor may threaten to lose their job or be demoted to ensure that a task is completed. This can be very stressful for the employee and negatively affect their mental health.

Control is another way that manipulation can occur in the workplace. This method aims to control the actions, decisions, or opinions of others. For example, a supervisor may try to control how an employee performs their work or influence their decisions. This can interfere with productivity and the employee's self-esteem.

Misinformation is a form of manipulation in which a person provides false or misleading information to influence the decisions of others. For example, a supervisor may provide false information about a project or an employee to influence the decisions of others. This can negatively impact productivity and team cohesion.

Manipulation in the workplace can also take the form of intimidation or bullying. This can occur when a person uses their position of power or their personality to threaten or intimidate others. This can negatively affect the mental health and well-being of employees and impact productivity and teamwork.

It is important to speak with a supervisor or a representative from human resources to discuss inappropriate behavior to address manipulation in the workplace. It may also be advisable to seek support from a counselor or lawyer to protect one's rights in the workplace. Additionally, it is important to set clear boundaries with supervisors and communicate expectations for how work should be performed.

It is important to create a transparent and open work environment in which all employees feel respected and heard to prevent manipulation in the workplace. This can be achieved by promoting a culture of open communication, in which employees can freely express their opinions and thoughts without fear of retaliation. Transparency in communication and business decisions is critical to ensuring that all employees have access to the information they need to perform their work efficiently and are not excluded or disadvantaged by misleading information.

Furthermore, it is important for companies to establish clear and strict policies for the prevention of bullying and discrimination in the workplace. This may include establishing complaint procedures, educating employees about inappropriate behavior, and sanctioning such behaviors. These policies can help create a safe and welcoming work environment for all employees.

In addition, companies should also consider investing in training and development programs for employees to acquire the necessary skills to recognize and manage manipulation situations. These programs can teach employees how to handle conflict situations, communicate effectively, and establish healthy and respectful relationships with colleagues and superiors.

Finally, companies need to listen to and take employees' concerns regarding manipulation in the workplace seriously. This can be done through the establishment of feedback and evaluation mechanisms so that employees can report concerns anonymously and companies can quickly take action to resolve them.

In summary, workplace manipulation can negatively affect employees, team dynamics, and company productivity. However, with a culture of transparent communication, strict policies for preventing bullying and discrimination, training and development programs, and an active response to employees' concerns, companies can prevent or effectively manage this type of behavior and promote a healthy and positive work environment. It is also important for employees to feel that they have an open channel to report any problems or manipulate situations so that they can be promptly addressed and resolved.

Speech on the negative impact manipulation can have on work performance and employees' mental health.

Manipulation in the workplace can negatively impact employees' mental health and work performance. Firstly, manipulation can cause stress and anxiety for employees, which can interfere with their ability to focus on work and make effective decisions. This can, in turn, negatively impact their productivity and the quality of their work.

Additionally, manipulation can create a hostile and unwelcoming work environment, which can lead to a loss of motivation and a sense of isolation among employees. This can also increase the risk of mental health problems such as depression or anxiety.

Manipulation can also distort team dynamics and create tensions between employees. This can lead to a decrease in collaboration and communication, which can again negatively impact the productivity and quality of the team's work.

Finally, workplace manipulation can also negatively affect the company's reputation and relationships with customers, suppliers, and other stakeholders. This can negatively impact the company's reputation and its ability to attract and retain talent and customers.

In summary, workplace manipulation can have long-term negative effects on employees' mental health and work performance, team dynamics, and the company's reputation. It is important for companies to promote a culture of transparent communication and prevent bullying and discrimination through strict policies and training and development programs to prevent these negative impacts. Additionally, it is important for companies to actively listen to employee concerns and intervene quickly to resolve any issues.

Exercise: Identifying and Resolving Workplace Manipulation Issues

A useful exercise (for those with authority to do so) to identify and solve workplace manipulation problems is a work climate survey. This exercise involves asking employees to respond to an anonymous questionnaire about their work environment, including any manipulation problems they have experienced or observed.

Example questionnaire:

1. In the last 6 months, have you experienced or observed manipulative behavior in the workplace? Yes/No
2. If yes, please describe these manipulative behaviors.
3. Who was involved in these manipulative behaviors?
4. What were the negative consequences of these behaviors on your work and personal life?
5. What actions do you think could be taken to prevent or resolve these manipulative behaviors in the workplace?
6. Do you feel safe and supported in reporting these manipulative behaviors to the appropriate authorities? Yes/No

After collecting the survey results, companies can use the data collected to identify workplace manipulation problems and take action to resolve them. For example, if the results show that a particular employee is behaving manipulatively, the company can intervene to address the problem and prevent further damage. If the results indicate that employees do not feel safe in reporting these behaviors, the company can take action to strengthen the culture of safety in the workplace and ensure that employees have a safe channel to report any problems.

Identified Problems	Action Taken
Employee X's manipulative behavior	Intervention with Employee X to address the issue and prevent further harm
Employees do not feel safe reporting manipulative behavior	Implementation of a safety culture in the workplace and the creation of a secure channel to report any issues

7

Political and media manipulation

Political and media manipulation is a widespread problem that significantly impacts modern societies and people's lives. This phenomenon can take various forms but generally occurs when information is presented misleadingly or deceptively to influence public opinion or achieve a specific political or economic goal.

Political manipulation occurs when politicians, political organizations, or interest groups present misleading or deceptive information to influence voters' opinions and voting choices. This can be done through the distortion of facts, partial or selective presentation of information or the use of propaganda and marketing techniques.

Media manipulation, on the other hand, occurs when media present misleading or deceptive information to influence public opinion. This can be done through partial or selective reporting, presenting false or misleading information, or using propaganda and marketing techniques.

Political and media manipulation can significantly negatively affect modern societies, as it can interfere with an individual's ability to make informed decisions and actively participate in political and social life.

This can, in turn, have a negative impact on the quality of democracy and political stability.

Furthermore, political and media manipulation can create a distorted perception of reality and facts, which can negatively impact the quality of public discourse and the ability to effectively address social and political issues. This can also increase the risk of conflicts and political polarization.

Promoting a culture of transparency and accountability in political and media communication is important to avoid political and media manipulation problems. This can be achieved by promoting ethical and transparent standards in political and media communication and creating an independent monitoring system that can monitor and report misleading or fraudulent behavior.

In addition, training and education on political and media manipulation are crucial to help people recognize and resist this deceptive behavior. Media literacy training, which is the ability to critically analyze and understand media and information, is an important step in preventing media manipulation. Training on active citizenship and the rights and responsibilities of citizens in a democracy is equally important in preventing political manipulation. Furthermore, the active participation of citizens in political and social life through exercising their right to vote, participating in public debates, and peaceful protest initiatives can help prevent political and media manipulation.

Finally, it is important for the media to play an active role in preventing political and media manipulation. The media should strive to maintain high standards of integrity and transparency and provide complete and unbiased information to help citizens make informed decisions. The media should also be free and independent of political and economic influences and be able to exercise critical oversight over politicians and political organizations.

In summary, political and media manipulation is a serious problem that can significantly negatively impact modern societies. Continuous engagement from all parties involved, including citizens, media, politicians, and political organizations, is required to prevent this phenomenon. Only through a culture of transparency, accountability, and education can we ensure that political and media information is complete, accurate, and unbiased and that political and social decisions are based on an informed understanding of reality.

Analysis of how manipulation is used in the political and media sphere

Political and media manipulation is used in many different ways to influence public opinion and people's decisions. Here are some examples:

1. Distortion of facts: This involves the selective or partial presentation of information to influence public opinion. For example, a politician might only present part of the facts about a particular issue to support their position.
2. Propaganda: This involves the use of emotional and persuasive techniques to influence public opinion. For example, a politician might use strong slogans and imagery to create a positive perception of their position or party.
3. Media manipulation: This involves the manipulation of the media to influence public opinion. For example, an interest group might pay to run misleading ads or manipulate the content of news.
4. Political marketing: This involves the use of marketing techniques to influence public opinion. For example, a politician might use advertising to create a positive image of their party or to present their views in an appealing way.
5. Fake news: This involves the spread of false or misleading information to influence public opinion. For example, an interest group might spread fake news about a politician or a particular issue to influence elections or public perception.
6. Fake polls: This involves the manipulation of polls to influence public opinion. For example, an interest group might commission fake polls to make a particular position appear more popular than it actually is.
7. Gaslighting: This involves the manipulation of people's perception of reality. For example, a politician might

continuously deny the truth about a particular issue to confuse public opinion and make their positions appear correct.

8. Influencer marketing involves using influencers or public figures to promote a particular position or product. For example, an interest group might pay an influencer to promote a political position on social media.

9. Discrediting: This involves attacking the credibility of a person or group to influence public opinion. For example, a politician might attack the credibility of a journalist or expert to make their positions appear less valid.

10. Disinformation: This involves the spread of false or misleading information to influence public opinion. For example, an interest group might spread disinformation about a topic to influence public perception.

It is important for people to be aware of these manipulation methods and develop the ability to recognize and resist manipulation. There are some things that people can do to protect themselves from manipulation, such as:

1. Checking sources: It is important to check the information source and ensure it is reliable and impartial.

2. Recognizing propaganda: It is important to be able to recognize propaganda and emotional and persuasive techniques used to influence public opinion.

3. Developing a critical understanding of news: It is important to develop a critical understanding of news and analyze information from different perspectives to get a complete picture of reality.

These are just some examples of how manipulation is used in politics and media. People need to be aware of these methods and develop the ability to recognize and resist manipulation in order to make informed decisions and actively participate in political and social life.

A speech about the negative effects that manipulation can have on society and the formation of public opinions

Let's talk about the negative impacts of manipulation on society and the formation of public opinions. Manipulation in politics and media negatively impacts society and the formation of public opinions. Here are some of these impacts:

1. Harm to democracy: Manipulation can have a negative impact on democracy as it distorts the truth and makes it difficult for citizens to make informed decisions and participate actively in political life. Furthermore, it can lead to polarization of public opinions, which leads to divisions and makes it harder for people to work together towards a common goal.

2. Loss of trust in the media: Manipulation of the media can lead to a loss of trust in the media by the public. When people learn that the news they have read is manipulated or false, it becomes difficult for them to distinguish between reliable and unreliable sources. This can spread false news and undermine trust in the media's ability to inform the public correctly.

3. Polarization of society: Manipulation can lead to polarization of society, where people develop strong and opposing opinions on a topic. This can make it harder to work together towards a common goal and contribute to increased violence and intolerance.

4. Impacts on the formation of public opinion: Manipulation can have negative impacts on the formation of public opinion. When people are exposed to false or distorted information, it will be difficult for them to form an informed and well-founded opinion on a topic. Furthermore, manipulation can negatively impact people's ability to form their own opinions, as emotional and persuasive techniques can influence them.

5. Impacts on mental health: Manipulation can also have negative impacts on the mental health of the population. For example, media manipulation can spread false or alarming news that can cause anxiety and stress. Furthermore, manipulation can also make it difficult to distinguish truth from lies, leading to a loss

of trust and an increase in paranoia and mistrust toward institutions and sources of information. This can have a negative impact on the mental and psychological health of the population and contribute to problems such as anxiety, depression, and stress.

Manipulation can also make it difficult for people to form healthy and sound relationships with others, as false or distorted opinions about specific individuals or groups can influence them. This can lead to an increase in intolerance and discrimination, increasing the risk of social and racial conflicts.

In summary, manipulation can negatively impact democracy, the formation of public opinions, mental health, and social cohesion. It is important for people to learn to recognize manipulation and for the media to take greater responsibility in providing accurate information to the population.

Exercise: Critical evaluation of news and information provided by the media

The critical evaluation of news and information provided by the media is crucial to avoid the spread of false or manipulated information and to form informed and well-founded opinions. Here are some tips for critically evaluating news:

1. Check the source: Check the source of the news and the reputation of the information medium that provides it. Look for reliable and verifiable sources and make sure the source is trustworthy and well-informed.
2. Check the date: When the news was published and whether it is current. Old or outdated news may be obsolete or no longer relevant.
3. Check for objectivity: Check whether the news is objective or presents a biased viewpoint. News that presents a biased point of view may be manipulated or influenced by special interests.

4. Check secondary sources: Check whether reliable sources have reported the news and whether other media or reliable sources have verified the information.
5. Check for truthfulness: Check whether the news is true and whether the provided information is accurate. Look for reliable and verifiable sources that can confirm or refute the news.
6. Check for coherence: Check whether the news is consistent with previous information on the same topic and whether the provided information is logically connected. In general, it is important to be skeptical and critical of news and information provided by the media and always to verify the truthfulness and validity of the information before forming an opinion or spreading it to others.

Here is an example of how you could critically evaluate news and information provided by the media:

Evaluation criterion	Description
Source	Who produced or disseminated the news or information? Is the source trustworthy and unbiased?
Date	When was the news or information published? Could it be outdated or no longer relevant?
Evidence	Are there any evidence or secondary sources that support the news or information?
Content	Is the content of the news or information accurate, complete, and correct?
Perspective	Is the news or information presented fairly and without bias? Is a balanced view of the facts presented?
Public interest	Does the news or information concern important societal issues, or is it an insignificant matter?

By using these criteria, you can critically evaluate the news and information the media provides and determine if they are reliable and trustworthy. This is important to avoid being influenced by false or distorted news and to form informed and well-founded opinions.

8

The psychology behind manipulation

Manipulation is a complex phenomenon that involves a range of psychological factors. Manipulation can be understood as a form of influence that seeks to induce others to act in a manner consistent with the goals of the individual or group that is attempting to manipulate. Manipulation can take many different forms but typically involves selecting information, communicating information in a deceptive manner, and creating false perceptions. Let's explore the psychology behind manipulation in more detail.

One of the key psychological factors underlying manipulation is the need to control others. People who seek to manipulate others often have a strong need for control, and manipulation is one of the tactics at their disposal to gain this control. People who seek to manipulate others often have low self-esteem or a sense of insecurity and seek to mask these weaknesses by manipulating others.

Another psychological factor that plays a role in manipulation is the desire to gain advantages. People who seek to manipulate others often do so because they believe they will benefit from doing so. These benefits can include control over an individual or group, obtaining material benefits, or achieving personal goals. However, people who seek to manipulate others often do not consider the negative consequences of their actions which can cause long-term harm to themselves and others.

A third psychological factor that plays a role in manipulation is the desire to protect one's self-image. People who seek to manipulate others often do so because they believe that what they are trying to achieve would not be well-received by others if done openly and honestly. As a result, they use manipulation as a form of self-image protection. This can include creating a perception of oneself that is not accurate or communicating information deceptively.

A fourth psychological factor that plays a role in manipulation is the complexity of the world around us. People often feel overwhelmed by our complex and chaotic world and may try to simplify reality through manipulation. In other words, manipulation can simplify reality that people use to feel more comfortable and in control.

In summary, manipulation is a complex phenomenon involving various psychological factors. These factors include the need to control others, the desire for advantages, the desire to protect self-image, and the complexity of the world around us. Understanding the psychology behind manipulation is important for recognizing when someone is trying to manipulate us and developing our critical abilities. When we know why someone is trying to manipulate us, we can develop the necessary defenses to resist manipulation and protect ourselves and others.

One of the key defenses against manipulation is awareness of our emotions and thoughts. When we are aware of our emotional states and thoughts, we can recognize when someone is trying to manipulate us through our emotional vulnerability. Learning to manage our emotions and the ability to critically evaluate information are important steps in resisting manipulation.

Another way to protect oneself from manipulation is the ability to analyze information critically. When we are able to critically analyze information, we can identify when someone is attempting to manipulate our perception of reality. Identifying reliable sources of information and verifying the information we receive is an important skill that helps us develop greater awareness and understanding of the world around us.

Finally, the ability to communicate effectively is an important defense against manipulation. When we are able to communicate clearly and assertively, we can protect ourselves and others from manipulation. Learning to communicate effectively requires practice and experience, but it is a valuable skill that allows us to express our opinions and defend our rights.

In conclusion, manipulation is a complex phenomenon involving various psychological factors. Awareness of these factors helps us recognize when someone is attempting to manipulate us and develop the necessary defenses to resist manipulation. Developing our ability to critically analyze information, verify information, and communicate effectively are important skills that help us protect ourselves and others from manipulation.

Exploration of the motivations that drive people to manipulate others

Manipulation is a common tactic many people use to get what they want from others. However, the reasons why people manipulate others can vary depending on the circumstances and individuals involved. Here are some of the most common motivations that drive people to manipulate others:

1. Control: The main motivation that drives many people to manipulate others is the desire for control. This can be due to various factors, including personal insecurity, fear of the unknown, or the need to be in command. People who try to manipulate others often try to create a situation where they are in charge and can control the behavior of others.

2. Self-esteem: Another common motivation for manipulation is the desire to boost self-esteem. People with low self-esteem may try to manipulate others to feel more secure. In this case, manipulation may create a self-image that does not reflect

reality but helps fulfill the need to feel important and competent.

3. Personal gain: People who try to manipulate others often do so because they believe they can gain personal benefits. These benefits may include control over a person or group, obtaining material benefits, or achieving personal goals. However, people who try to manipulate others often do not consider the negative consequences of their actions and may cause long-term damage to themselves and others.

4. Respect: Some people try to manipulate others because they want to be respected and admired by others. This type of manipulation often relies on creating a self-image that does not reflect reality but helps to gain the respect of others. In this case, manipulation may be used to conceal personal weaknesses and create a self-image that appears strong and confident.

5. Fear: Finally, fear can drive some people to manipulate others. People who are afraid may try to manipulate others to create a situation where they feel safer and more protected. In this case, manipulation may be used to avoid dangerous or unfamiliar situations.

In summary, the motivations that drive people to manipulate others can vary depending on the circumstances and people involved. However, the most common motivations for manipulation are the desire for control, increasing self-esteem, personal benefits, respect, and fear. Understanding these motivations can help recognize, avoid manipulation, and avoid falling into manipulation traps.

Analysis of the psychological techniques used by manipulators

Manipulators use a variety of psychological techniques to influence and control others. These techniques can be subtle or obvious, but they all aim to manipulate the perceptions and behaviors of others. Here are some of the most common techniques used by manipulators:

1. Praise: Manipulators may start praising and congratulating the person they want to manipulate to create a sense of mutual

respect and emotional openness. This can lower the individual's defensiveness and make them more willing to accept the manipulator's requests.

2. Isolation: Manipulators may try to isolate the person they want to manipulate from family, friends, or the outside world to limit access to alternative sources of information and social support. This way, the individual can become more dependent on the manipulator, who becomes the only source of approval, support, and information.

3. Fear: Manipulators can use fear to make people do what they want. They can threaten to reveal secrets, make embarrassing or compromising information public, or damage the individual's reputation or career. This can make the individual give in to the manipulator's demands to avoid negative consequences.

4. Persuasion: Manipulators can use persuasion and rhetoric to make people do what they want. They can use logical arguments, statistics, anecdotes, and other rhetorical tools to convince the individual of their point of view and act accordingly.

5. Guilt: Manipulators may try to make the individual they want to manipulate feel guilty by exploiting their emotional weaknesses. They can express guilt for lack of attention, concerns, or responsibilities toward others or for anything that makes them individual feel inadequate. This way, manipulators can force individuals to do what they want by exploiting their vulnerability.

6. Confusion: Manipulators can use confusion to create a sense of insecurity and disorientation in the people they want to manipulate. They can present conflicting or ambiguous information or frequently change their attitude or requests. This can make the individual feel confused and concerned, making them more willing to accept the manipulator's requests.

7. Seduction: Manipulators can use seduction to induce people to do what they want. They can flirt and use physical

attractiveness or personal charm to create a sense of connection and desire in the individual, making them more susceptible to the manipulator's demands.

8. Control: Manipulators may try to control the environment and situations in which the people they want to manipulate limit their options and ability to make autonomous decisions. For example, they may create situations where the individual needs their help or guidance or limit access to resources or information necessary for autonomous decision-making.

9. Intimidation: Manipulators may use threats or physical violence to force people to do what they want. This technique is very aggressive and often illegal, but unfortunately, some manipulators use it to get what they want.

10. Emotional manipulation: Manipulators may use emotional manipulation to exploit the individual's emotions and make them act against their own interests. For example, they may bring out the individual's anger, sadness, or fear in order to convince them to do what they want.

It is important to note that many of these techniques are used subtly and insidiously. Often, the manipulated individual does not realize what is happening until it is too late. Additionally, manipulators may use different techniques in combination with each other to increase the likelihood that their manipulation is successful. Awareness of these techniques is the first step in preventing manipulation and protecting one's autonomy and individual freedom.

Exercise: Understanding the motivations and psychological techniques used by manipulators

Exercise: Understanding the motivations and psychological techniques manipulators use can involve various activities. Below, I propose a possible exercise: Analysis of a manipulation case:

1. Carefully read the following case:

- Sarah and Luke are co-workers. Sarah has always disliked Luke because she considers him too ambitious and ready to trample on others to achieve his goals. One day, Luke organizes a dinner at his house and invites all his colleagues from the office, including Sarah. During the evening, Luke is very friendly with Sarah and constantly tries to involve her in interesting conversations. At the end of the dinner, Sarah feels very comfortable with Luke and thinks that her opinion of him may have changed. However, in the following days, Sarah notices that Luke has started ignoring her again at the office and continues behaving as if nothing had happened. Sarah is confused and disappointed and wonders if Luke manipulated her to achieve his goals.

2. Answer the following questions:

- What could be Luke's motivations for manipulating Sarah?
- What psychological techniques could he have used to manipulate her?
- How could Sarah defend herself against possible manipulation in the future?

3. Reflect on the answers to the previous questions, and try to get a different perspective, if possible, by having a friend or someone else answer the questions. Then discuss possible solutions to the problem.

This activity can help develop critical thinking and an understanding of the motivations and psychological techniques used by manipulators. Additionally, it can provide students with useful tools to defend themselves against possible manipulations in the future.

Here is a table that lists the motivations and psychological techniques used by manipulators:

Motivations	Psychological techniques used
Control	Gaslighting, denial of reality, isolation, intimidation
Self-esteem	Love bombing, flattery, excessive appreciation, destructive criticism, invalidation
Personal benefit	Manipulation of information, coercion, threats, blackmail
Power and status	Humiliation, dehumanization, domination, exploitation, distortion of the truth
Narcissism	Projection, gaslighting, invalidation, destructive criticism, excessive emphasis on self-image

It's important to note that manipulators' motivations and psychological techniques can vary significantly depending on the individual and specific situation. This table only provides a general idea of manipulators' most common motivations and techniques.

9

Developing resilience against manipulation

Developing resilience against manipulation can be difficult, but it is possible with the right attention and dedication. Below are some tips that can help:

1. Know yourself: It's important to first understand your emotions, limits, and values. Knowing yourself makes it easier to recognize when something or someone is trying to manipulate you.
2. Learn to recognize manipulation: Familiarize yourself with the most common manipulation techniques, such as guilt, shame, and isolation. Learn to recognize when someone is trying to manipulate you and be prepared to respond.
3. Learn to say "no": Learn to say no to unreasonable demands and undue pressure. Don't feel guilty for saying no - it's your right and responsibility to protect yourself.
4. Build a support network: Having friends and family members you can trust can help you resist manipulation. Seek support from people who love and support you.
5. Seek professional help: If you are experiencing a persistent or extreme situation of manipulation, seek help from a professional such as a therapist. A professional can help you

develop strategies to resist manipulation and build greater resilience.

6. Maintain your independence: Try to maintain your independence and autonomy in all situations. Don't give up your freedom of choice and decision for anyone.
7. Practice self-care: Take care of yourself and your mental and emotional well-being. Learn to manage stress and negative emotions and try to maintain a healthy and balanced lifestyle.
8. Be assertive: Be assertive and defend your rights and values. Don't force anyone to force you to do something you don't want to or think in a certain way.

Developing resilience against manipulation takes time and effort, but it can help protect your mental and emotional health and lead to a more authentic and satisfying life. These are all great tips for developing resilience against manipulation.

Here are some key points that can help you implement them in your daily life:

1. Be self-aware: Reflect on yourself, your emotions, and your values. This will help you build greater awareness of what you want and don't want in your life.
2. Be vigilant: Be aware of their attitudes and behaviors when interacting with others. Notice if there are repeated patterns of manipulation and, if so, try to recognize them and respond appropriately.
3. Practice: Put into practice the art of saying no to unreasonable requests and undue pressures. Don't be afraid to defend your boundaries and your rights.
4. Seek support from trusted individuals: Having a support network of friends and family who support and encourage you is essential for developing resilience against manipulation.
5. Seek professional help: If the situation of manipulation is particularly difficult, seek the help of a professional. A therapist can help you develop strategies to resist manipulation and build greater resilience.

6. Seek your independence: Seek to maintain your independence and autonomy in every situation. Don't allow anyone to control you or force you to do something you don't want to do.

7. Practice self-care: Take care of yourself on a regular basis. Learn to manage stress and negative emotions and strive to maintain a balanced lifestyle.

8. Be assertive: Be assertive in defending your rights and values. Don't allow anyone to make you feel guilty for who you are or what you want. I would also like to add that it's important to be patient and kind to yourself during this process. Resisting manipulation can be difficult, and you shouldn't feel guilty if you struggle to consistently apply these suggestions.

Additionally, it's important to be open to change and continuous learning, as manipulation can take many different forms, and new techniques may emerge over time. With practice and consistent effort, it's possible to develop resilience against manipulation and live a more authentic and fulfilling life.

A speech about techniques to strengthen self-esteem and self-awareness

Self-esteem and self-awareness are fundamental aspects of psychological well-being and success in life. Many techniques can help improve these aspects, and many of them are based on self-awareness and practicing positive thinking.

Here are some techniques that can be useful for strengthening one's self-esteem and self-awareness:

1. Work on emotional awareness: Emotional awareness is recognizing and understanding one's emotional states. Practicing emotional awareness can help one better understand oneself and increase self-esteem. People can practice emotional awareness by dedicating time every day to reflect on their emotional state and the situations that provoke them.

2. Learn to say no: Saying no when necessary is important to maintain balance and respect one's limits. Learning to say no to situations that make us feel uncomfortable or stressed can help develop a sense of control over one's life and improve self-esteem.

3. Identify and challenge negative thoughts: Often, negative thoughts can influence self-esteem. Learning to recognize one's negative thoughts and challenge them with positive thoughts can help strengthen self-esteem and have a more balanced view of oneself.

4. Seek support from others: Talking to friends, family, or a mental health professional can help improve self-esteem. Having someone who listens and supports us can be an important factor in increasing self-confidence.

5. Practice self-care: Taking care of oneself physically, emotionally, and mentally can help strengthen self-esteem. Exercise, getting enough sleep, eating a healthy and balanced diet, and engaging in hobbies that we enjoy are all ways to take care of ourselves.

6. Try new activities and challenges: Trying new and challenging things can help develop a sense of competence and increase self-esteem. Trying a new hobby, learning a new skill, or participating in a social event are all activities that can help develop self-esteem.

Additionally, it's important to remember that improving self-esteem and self-awareness requires time and commitment. Working on these aspects requires continuous effort, but the benefits can be significant.

In fact, improving self-esteem and self-awareness requires consistent commitment and a willingness to invest time and energy in oneself. It's also important to understand that every individual is unique, and there is no one-size-fits-all solution. Therefore, exploring different techniques and finding the ones that work best for oneself is important.

I would also add that keeping a journal is another useful technique for strengthening self-esteem and self-awareness. Writing down one's thoughts and emotions can help to better understand oneself and identify one's thoughts and behavior patterns.

Additionally,, tracking progress can be a way to strengthen self-esteem. Another useful technique focuses on strengths and successes rather than weaknesses and failures. Trying to find at least one positive thing about oneself daily can help change one's perspective and develop a more positive attitude toward oneself.

Finally, another important aspect to consider is the practice of gratitude. Being grateful for what one has in life can help to develop a more positive and thankful attitude toward oneself and others. Additionally, practicing gratitude can help to focus on the positive things in life and develop greater emotional resilience.

Exercise: Developing resilience through meditation and self-esteem enhancement techniques

Guided gratitude meditation is an exercise that can help develop resilience through meditation techniques and self-confidence building. This exercise can help develop an awareness of one's own thoughts and emotions, improve the ability to cope with them, and maintain a positive attitude even in difficult situations. Here's how to do the exercise:

1. Find a quiet place where you can sit or lie down comfortably.
2. Focus on your breathing and inhale and exhale slowly and deeply.
3. After a few minutes, focus on a positive thought, such as a happy moment or a recent achievement.
4. Imagine that you are grateful for this moment or achievement and try to visualize as many details as possible.
5. Continue to breathe slowly and deeply while focusing on gratitude and the positive feeling it gives you.
6. If your mind becomes distracted or deviates from the positive thought, gently return to the gratitude visualization.
7. Continue the guided gratitude meditation for a few minutes, breathing slowly and focusing on the feeling of gratitude and happiness it gives you.

Regularly repeating this exercise can help develop the ability to concentrate on positive thoughts and emotions and strengthen self-confidence and resilience.

Another exercise for developing resilience through meditation techniques and boosting self-confidence could be the practice of gratitude. Gratitude is an attitude of appreciation and recognition for the good things in life. The practice of gratitude can help develop a sense of positivity and appreciation for what one has rather than focusing on what is lacking or not going well.

Here are some ways to practice gratitude as an exercise for developing resilience:

1. Take time every day to think about the things you are grateful for: You can choose to do this in the morning before starting your day or at night before going to bed. Write down in a notebook or journal the things you are grateful for and focus on what you have rather than what you lack.
2. Create a list of three things you are grateful for. Every day, create a list of three things you are grateful for and write them down in a notebook or journal. It doesn't matter if they are big or small things: focusing on what you have and appreciating it is important.

The practice of gratitude can help develop resilience by helping you focus on the positive aspects of life, even in difficult times. It can also help improve self-esteem by encouraging you to acknowledge the good things in your life and develop a sense of appreciation for yourself and your accomplishments.

10

Manipulation in digital life

Manipulation in digital life is a common practice involving psychological techniques to influence people to do something or have certain thoughts or behaviors. In many cases, manipulation occurs through the use of subliminal persuasion techniques, where people are not aware of the influence they are experiencing. Here are some examples of manipulation in digital life:

1. Creating addiction: Many apps and websites are designed to create addiction in users, making them compulsively return to use them. Likes, notifications, and update alerts can become sources of gratification that drive people to use the platform more and more.
2. Creating false hopes: In many cases, online advertising and marketing campaigns create false hopes in consumers, making them believe that a certain product or service can solve all their problems or fulfill all their desires. In reality, these ads are often exaggerated or misleading.
3. Creating a false identity: People can manipulate their online image to create a false identity, making others believe they are someone they are not. This can be done through the use of fake images or by creating fake profiles on social media.

4. Creating false urgency: Many online marketing campaigns try to create false urgency, pushing people to act immediately so as not to miss an opportunity or take advantage of a limited-time offer. In reality, these offers are often not as advantageous as they seem and can lead to unnecessary expenses.

It is important to develop greater awareness of the techniques used and learn to recognize them to protect oneself from manipulation in digital life. It is also important to take control of one's digital life and use online platforms consciously rather than being controlled by them.

Manipulation in digital life has become increasingly common due to the widespread use of technology, the internet, and social media. Users are often exposed to subtle persuasion techniques and psychological manipulation that can influence their thoughts, behaviors, and decisions.

Another example of manipulation in digital life is the phenomenon of fake news, which refers to false or misleading news spread through social media and other online channels. These news items often attempt to influence public opinion on political, social, and cultural issues by convincing people to believe certain ideologies or take positions that may not be based on reality. The spread of fake news is particularly concerning as it can negatively impact democracy and social cohesion.

Another example of manipulation in digital life concerns privacy and the collection of personal data. Many companies use tracking and profiling techniques to gather information about users' online activities, interests, and behaviors. This information can be used to create personalized advertising or sell personal data to third parties, which poses a risk to users' privacy and security.

It is important to develop a greater awareness of the techniques used and learn how to recognize them to protect oneself from manipulation in digital life. For example, users should carefully scrutinize the online news and information they read to verify their source and veracity. Additionally, it is important to read online platforms' privacy policies and limit personal information sharing.

Furthermore, users should try not to become overly reliant on technology and online platforms and use them consciously and in a balanced manner. For example, users can set time limits for social media and online browsing and focus on activities that promote well-being and mental health.

Finally, institutions and regulatory authorities should take measures to protect users from manipulation in digital life, such as by enacting rules for online advertising and collecting personal data.

Analysis of how manipulation is used in the digital world, such as on social media and the internet

Manipulation in the digital world is becoming increasingly widespread, especially on social media and the internet. This is because social media has become an integral part of many people's daily lives, and many activities and interactions occur online. People often rely on these channels for information, entertainment, connection with friends and family, and discovering new products and services.

However, this digital environment can be highly manipulative. For example, social media uses sophisticated algorithms to control what users see in their feeds, creating a kind of filter bubble. This means that users may be exposed only to news and information confirming their views while ignoring conflicting news and opinions. This can contribute to polarization and the increase of intolerance between people, especially in political or social contexts.

Additionally, manipulation can also occur through online advertising. Advertising on social media and search engines is often designed to grab the user's attention and prompt them to take a specific action, such as clicking on an ad or purchasing a product. These ads can be highly targeted based on information about user behaviors, such as interests and preferences.

Manipulation can also occur through comments and discussions on social media. Users may use persuasion techniques to convince others to share their opinions, such as using emotional arguments or attempting to invalidate the opinions of others. Furthermore, online anonymity can lead people to behave aggressively and rudely without the social consequences that would occur in a face-to-face context.

Finally, manipulation can occur through creating fake profiles on social media or disseminating false or misleading news. This can be done to influence users' opinions or spread hate or disinformation.

It is important to develop a greater awareness of the techniques used and learn to recognize them to avoid online manipulation. Additionally, it is important to take control of one's digital life and use online platforms consciously rather than being controlled by them. Users should be cautious when providing personal information online and use privacy tools to limit data collection. Finally, users should also verify online information sources and consider their credibility before sharing them with others.

In addition to individual awareness, it is important for online platforms to take greater responsibility in preventing manipulation. There have been various initiatives to regulate online advertising and limit the spread of fake news, but much work still needs to be done. Platforms should take responsibility for identifying and removing manipulative content and ensuring greater transparency in the use of user data.

Furthermore, digital education and skill development are critical to helping people understand the implications of the digital world and develop the necessary skills to use it safely and responsibly. There should be a greater focus on teaching young people how to evaluate online sources and recognize and resist manipulation. Adults should also be encouraged to participate in training programs and develop a greater awareness of the impact of technology on their lives.

Finally, it is important to recognize that online manipulation is not just a technological problem but also a broader social and political problem. Online polarization and intolerance reflect deeper problems in society, such as inequality and a lack of dialogue and understanding between different groups. Preventing online manipulation, therefore, requires a broader and global response involving not only online platforms but also governments, civil society organizations, and citizens themselves.

A speech about the negative impact manipulation can have on digital life.

Manipulation in the digital world can have many negative impacts on users' lives and society as a whole. Firstly, it can affect users' perception of reality. When users are only exposed to information and opinions that confirm their pre-existing beliefs, it can become difficult to distinguish reality from personal opinion. This can lead to an increase in polarization and intolerance, where people become less willing to listen to and consider the opinions of others, causing social and political divisions.

Additionally, manipulation can lead to the spread of false or misleading information. This can happen when users are intentionally exposed to inaccurate or misleading news and information that may appear credible. This can lead to the dissemination of misinformation and conspiracy theories, which can negatively affect citizens' health and safety.

Manipulation can also lead to privacy and security issues. When users provide personal information online, they can become vulnerable to identity theft, financial fraud, and other types of fraudulent activity. Additionally, when users' data is collected and used without their consent, they can feel their privacy is violated.

Online manipulation can also lead to mental health issues. When exposed to violent or offensive content on social media or other online channels, users can develop anxiety, depression, and other psychological disorders. Additionally, anonymity online can lead people to behave aggressively and rudely, causing harm to others' mental health.

Finally, online manipulation can also have political consequences. When social media is used to influence elections or spread misleading or false political messages, it can result in a distortion of the democratic process. This can lead to an increase in political polarization, voter apathy, and a loss of trust in institutions.

In summary, manipulation in the digital world can have many negative consequences on users' lives and society. Users need to be aware of the techniques used and make informed choices to protect their privacy, mental health, and participation in political decisions.

It is important to note that online manipulation can take many forms, from manipulating information on social media to targeted advertising and spamming. And while the negative impact on digital life is apparent, online manipulation can also have negative consequences in real life. For example, the spread of misinformation about vaccinations can lead to an increase in infectious diseases, while false news about elections can undermine political stability and trust in institutions. Additionally, it is important to note that online manipulation occurs through social media and through other online platforms such as discussion forums, emails, and websites. For example, sending phishing emails that try to convince users to provide personal or financial information is fraudulent and can cause financial damage and compromise user security.

In conclusion, online manipulation is an increasingly widespread and complex problem requiring a multidisciplinary approach. Private companies that manage online platforms can also play an important role in combating online manipulation. For example, platforms can introduce algorithms to identify and remove false and misleading content and bots that spread false messages. Additionally, platforms can introduce greater controls on online advertising to prevent the spread of political messages or fraudulent products.

Finally, users themselves can do their part to protect themselves and society from online manipulation. Users can learn to recognize online manipulation techniques and adopt safe online behavior. For example, users can avoid providing personal or financial information online, use antivirus software and a firewall to protect their data, and verify the sources of information before sharing it on social media.

In summary, online manipulation is an increasingly common and complex societal threat. However, through an integrated approach involving public authorities, private companies, and users themselves, it is possible to combat online manipulation and protect our privacy, mental health, and participation in political decisions.

Exercise: Identifying and Solving Manipulation Problems in Digital Life

Here's an example exercise on identifying and solving manipulation problems in digital life:

1. Identify an example of online manipulation you have encountered recently. It could be a misleading advertisement, fake news article, spam message, or offensive comment.
2. Describe the manipulation problem and its consequences. What false or misleading information are they trying to make you believe? How could this affect your behavior or opinions?
3. Identify possible sources of manipulation. Who is trying to manipulate you, and why? What are their interests and motivations? Are they able to benefit from your gullibility or behavior?
4. Evaluate the accuracy of the information. Do research to verify the information that has been provided to you. Look for reliable sources and verify information from more than one source.
5. Take the necessary steps to protect yourself. If you have identified manipulation, take the necessary steps to protect yourself. For example, you could block the author of the offensive comment, report the misleading advertisement, or report the fake news article.
6. Share your experience with others. Share your experience of manipulation with others to raise awareness of the issue. You can do this on social media, talk to friends, or share your story online.
7. Be critical and attentive in the future. Be critical and attentive when encountering information online. Ask questions and verify sources before believing anything. This way, you will be able to protect yourself from manipulation and its negative consequences.

Example for identifying and solving manipulation problems in digital life:

Manipulation Issue	Identification	Solution
Spread of vaccine misinformation	Users are exposed to false and misleading information that can negatively influence their decision to get vaccinated.	Provide accurate, scientifically-based information on vaccinations and the diseases they prevent; actively combat online misinformation through educational campaigns and messages from health experts.
Misleading targeted advertising	Online advertising is presented in a misleading or deceptive manner to encourage users to take actions they would not otherwise take.	Regulate online advertising practices and require that ads be clearly labeled as such; educate users on how to recognize advertising and understand targeting practices.
Cyberbullying and trolling	People use online anonymity to attack and harass others.	Promote an online culture of respect and tolerance; educate users on cyber bullying and trolling and report to relevant authorities.
Online election manipulation	External actors use social media to spread false or misleading political messages to influence elections.	Regulate the use of social media in politics; actively combat online misinformation through educational campaigns and messages from political experts.
Collection and use of user data without consent	Companies collect and use user data for unclear or unauthorized purposes.	Regulate online use and collection of user data; require companies to provide clear information to consumers on the collection and use of their data and obtain their explicit consent before using their data.
Spread of online conspiracy theories	Users are exposed to conspiracy theories that can negatively influence their perception of reality.	Promote an online culture based on truth and evidence; educate users on conspiracy theories and understand the dangers of their online spread.

Manipulation Issue	Identification	Solution

11

Body language and nonverbal communication

Body language and nonverbal communication are important tools for expressing emotions and interacting with others. This form of communication refers to all nonverbal signals, such as body posture, gestures, facial expressions, and the use of space that can convey implicit meanings during a conversation. Nonverbal communication can influence the perception others have of us and provide information about our personality, emotional states, and intentions.

Facial expressions are a common example of nonverbal communication. A smile is often considered a sign of happiness and well-being, while a frowning face can suggest disapproval or anger. People we meet in daily life often use facial expressions to convey information about their emotional state and communicate with others without using words.

Body posture and gestures can also influence the perception of others. A person who sits up straight and has an open posture may be perceived as more confident and self-assured than someone who has a slouched posture and lowers their gaze. Gestures can also emphasize the meaning of what is being said. For example, touching the shoulder can signal empathy or compassion.

Space and distance between people can also convey information about their relationship and the level of comfort they have with each other. For example, the distance between people during a conversation can indicate their relationship: people who stand very close to each other can be more intimate and comfortable with each other than those who keep a greater distance.

Nonverbal communication can also provide clues about people's intentions. For example, avoiding direct eye contact can indicate that a person is hiding something or has something to hide. On the other hand, prolonged eye contact can signal interest and engagement.

Body language and nonverbal communication are important for our social and psychological well-being. They can help improve our communication skills and enhance our relationships with others. For example, appropriate posture, eye contact, and gestures can help create an image of self-assurance and confidence.

However, body language and nonverbal communication can also be used to manipulate others, such as in the political or advertising industry. It is, therefore, important to recognize manipulation techniques and protect oneself from the negative effects of nonverbal communication.

In summary, nonverbal communication is important to our daily lives and social relationships. It can convey implicit meanings and influence the perception others to have of us by providing information about our personality, emotional state, and intentions. Body posture, gestures, facial expressions, and the use of space are just a few examples of nonverbal communication that can be used to improve our communication skills and relationships with others. However, it is important to be aware of possible manipulation techniques through nonverbal communication and protect oneself from the negative effects.

Furthermore, nonverbal communication can vary depending on culture, age, and social context. This means that the same facial expressions or gestures may have different meanings in different parts of the world or in different situations. For example, prolonged eye contact may be seen as rude or aggressive in some cultures, while it is a sign of respect and interest in others.

Additionally, age can influence people's nonverbal communication. Small children may be more expressive and use gestures and facial expressions more than adults, while older people may be more reserved and use fewer gestures. Social context can also influence nonverbal communication: in a formal environment, such as a job interview, body posture, and eye contact may be more rigid than in an informal setting, such as a meeting with friends.

Finally, our nonverbal communication can be influenced by our emotional state. For example, a nervous or insecure person may show signs of stress, such as leg movements or sweaty hands, while a happy person may smile more and move more fluidly. It is important to be aware of these nonverbal signals and understand how they can affect our communication with others.

In summary, nonverbal communication is a complex and versatile aspect of our social interaction. It is important to understand how it works and can be used to improve our relationships with others, but also to be aware of the potential risks of manipulation. Decoding the nonverbal signals of others and using nonverbal communication effectively and consciously can make a difference in creating meaningful and lasting connections with others.

Introduction to Body Language and Nonverbal Communication

Nonverbal communication is the process of communicating using gestures, facial expressions, posture, and other body signals to convey emotions, thoughts, and intentions without words. Body language is one of the most powerful means of communicating with others, as gestures and expressions convey strong and immediate meanings.

Body language may include gestures such as waving hands, crossing arms, stomping feet, or nodding the head. Facial expressions can include smiling, widening eyes, furrowing brows, and pursed lips. Posture can convey emotions such as insecurity, confidence, or relaxation.

Nonverbal communication is important because it often conveys more accurate information about a person's emotions and intentions than the words themselves. For example, a person may say they are happy, but if their facial expression and tone of voice suggest otherwise, nonverbal communication indicates that they are actually unhappy.

It is important to be aware of one's body language and that of others to communicate effectively. Awareness of one's body language can help convey one's message more clearly and establish a stronger connection with others. Reading the body language of others can help to better understand their feelings and intentions and communicate more effectively.

In summary, body language and nonverbal communication are essential human communication elements and can convey strong and immediate meanings. Awareness of one's body language and that of others is important for communicating effectively and building a stronger connection.

Finally, body language and nonverbal communication are universal and transcend linguistic and cultural barriers. Some gestures and facial expressions are recognized worldwide as symbols of common emotions and intentions. For example, a smile is universally recognized as a sign of happiness, while furrowed eyebrows can signal concern or disapproval. Understanding these signals can be helpful when communicating with people from different cultures and languages.

Analysis of body language signals and their interpretation

Interpreting body language signals can help to better understand the emotions, intentions, and thoughts of the person you are communicating with. However, it should be emphasized that interpreting signals is not an exact science and can be subjective, influenced by factors such as culture, personal experience, and the context in which communication occurs.

Furthermore, analyzing body language signals and their interpretation can be a complex and detailed process, as many different signals can convey a wide range of meanings. Some of the most common body language signals and their possible interpretations include:

1. Facial expressions: Facial expressions are one of the most obvious body language signals and can convey a wide range of emotions. For example, a smile can indicate happiness, joy, or satisfaction, while a grimace can indicate sadness, anger, or disappointment.
2. Posture: Posture can provide information about a person's mood and confidence. An upright and open posture can indicate confidence, while a hunched and closed posture can indicate insecurity or shyness.
3. Hand gestures: Hand gestures can indicate nervousness, frustration, or uncertainty. For example, a person may touch or rub their hands when they are nervous or anxious.
4. Eye contact: Eye contact can indicate interest, attention, or nervousness. A person who maintains eye contact can indicate interest or attention, while a person who avoids eye contact may indicate nervousness or insecurity.
5. Leg movements: Leg movements can provide information about a person's comfort level. For example, leg tapping can indicate nervousness or irritability, while a comfortable leg position can indicate relaxation or satisfaction.
6. Voice expressions: Voice expressions can provide information about a person's emotions. For example, a monotone voice can indicate boredom or fatigue, while an energetic tone can indicate enthusiasm or interest.
7. Facial and body expressions: Facial and body expressions can provide information about a person's emotional state. For example, chest expansion and an upright posture can indicate confidence, while someone crossing their arms and legs can indicate insecurity or defensiveness.
8. Touch: Touch can indicate affection, interest, or attention. For example, a hug can indicate affection or interest, while a firm handshake can indicate trust or determination.

It is important to note that the same expression or gesture can have different meanings depending on the cultural or situational context in which it is used. For example, a smile can be interpreted differently in different cultures or situations, such as in a work context or informal social context. Additionally, it is important to analyze body language signals in the overall context of communication and not just rely on interpreting a single isolated signal. Finally, it is important to emphasize that understanding and interpreting body language should not be used to judge or label people but rather to better understand their emotions and intentions and improve interpersonal communication and relationships.

However, the ability to interpret body language can be useful in social and interpersonal situations and professional contexts such as negotiations, job interviews, or public presentations. Recognizing the body language signals of others and controlling one's own signals can increase communicative effectiveness and improve the ability to influence others.

It is also important to note that body language is only one part of communication. It is important to listen to people's words and consider the context in which the communication is taking place to understand the message completely.

Finally, while learning to interpret body language through practice and study is possible, it is important not to fall into the trap of making excessive or hasty assumptions or interpretations. It is important to remember that each person is unique and that body language signals can have many nuances and different meanings.

Exercise: Identifying Body Language Signals in Everyday Communication

The exercise of identifying body language signals in everyday communication can help develop observation and interpretation skills for nonverbal signals. Here are some tips for practicing:

1. Observe facial expressions: During a conversation, try to notice the facial expressions of the person you are speaking with. What might their smile or frown indicate? Do they appear happy or sad?

2. Observe posture: Note the person's posture. Are they sitting upright or slouching? Are their arms crossed or open? Do they appear relaxed or tense?
3. Observe hand movements: Observe the person's hand movements while you're talking. Are they rubbing their hands or playing with their fingers? It could be a sign of anxiety or boredom.
4. Observe eye contact: Pay attention to eye contact. Does the person look directly into your eyes or avoid eye contact? What could it mean?
5. Observe leg movements: Notice the person's leg movements. Are they moving nervously or relaxed? It could be a sign of discomfort or well-being.
6. Observe vocal expressions: Pay attention to the person's tone of voice. Is it monotone or energetic? Do they seem interested or bored?
7. Observe facial and body expressions: Notice the person's facial and body expressions. Are they expanding or contracting? Are they open or closed? What can it indicate?
8. Observe touch: Pay attention to gestures of physical contact. Does the person hug you or give you a pat on the shoulder? It could be a sign of affection or friendship.

Remember that the interpretation of body language signals can be subjective and influenced by various factors. Do not try to judge or label the person based on their nonverbal cues but use your observation to improve your understanding and relationship with others.

Example of identifying body language signals in everyday communication:

Situation	Body language signal	Possible interpretation
During a job interview	Keeps looking at the clock	Lack of interest or nervousness
A friend	Covers her mouth while laughing	Shyness or an awkward situation
During a heated discussion	Crosses their arms over their chest	Defensiveness or mental closure
A person	Holds their arms open and smiles while listening to a friend	Openness and interest
During a presentation	Speaks softly and doesn't move much	Nervousness or fear of public speaking
In a group of friends	Turns slightly to another and tilts their head while speaking	Interest and engagement in the conversation
During a romantic dinner	Touches their partner's arm gently	Affection and attention
In a business meeting	Scratches their head or touches their face	Worry or uncertainty
During a class	Yawns repeatedly	Tiredness or boredom
In a conversation with a doctor	Stares intensely at the floor	Nervousness or discomfort

Exercise

Situation	Body language signal	Possible interpretation

Situation	Body language signal	Possible interpretation

Situation	Body language signal	Possible interpretation

12

The body language in manipulation

Body language can be used to manipulate people, for example, in situations where one wants to convince someone to do something or believe in something that is not true. For instance, a person can use body language to appear more convincing or credible than they actually are. Here are some examples of how body language can be used for manipulation:

- Maintaining constant eye contact: Maintaining constant eye contact can be used to convey a sense of security and confidence and make one's message appear more credible. However, it can also be used to manipulate or intimidate the person one is speaking with.
- Exaggerated gestures: Using exaggerated and theatrical gestures can be used to emphasize a point and make one's message appear more important than it actually is. This can be used to manipulate the emotions and reactions of the person one is speaking with.
- Avoiding eye contact: Avoiding eye contact can be used to make a person appear less confident and less credible. This can be used to manipulate the other person's perception of one's authority and competence.

- Using a dominant posture: A dominant posture, such as crossing one's arms or standing over a person, can be used to manipulate or intimidate the person one is speaking with.
- Using ambivalent facial expressions: Using ambivalent facial expressions can be used to confuse or manipulate the person one is speaking with. For example, a false smile can be used to suggest that one is saying something positive when one actually means something negative.
- Changing one's tone of voice: Changing one's tone of voice can be used to convey different emotions and influence the other person's perception of one's credibility and authority.

In general, it is important to be aware of how one's body language can influence the emotions and perceptions of others. However, it is also important to be able to recognize and resist the manipulation of body language by others.

Body language can be a powerful tool of persuasion and manipulation, but it is also important to note that it can be easily misunderstood or misinterpreted. Nonverbal communication can be influenced by many factors, including culture, environment, and the context of the situation.

Furthermore, body language should never be used to manipulate or deceive people. Honesty and transparency are crucial for effective communication and building trust relationships. Body language manipulation can lead to a loss of trust and respect and ultimately damage interpersonal relationships.

However, there are also cases where body language can be used to help build positive relationships and improve communication. For example, appropriate eye contact and an open posture can help others feel heard and understood.

The importance of body language is also evident in professional contexts, such as the workplace. People who are able to master body language may have a greater likelihood of success in the workplace, as they can convey confidence and authority and increase their influence and persuasion.

However, body language should never be used to manipulate or harm others. Instead, it should be used to create positive connections and improve communication. It is also important to note that body language should not be the only form of communication used. Nonverbal communication should always be used with verbal communication to ensure the message is correctly understood.

In summary, body language is an important aspect of human communication and can be used to influence the emotions and perceptions of others. However, it is important to use it ethically and responsibly and always respect others. Being aware of one's own body language and how it is perceived by others is crucial to building positive interpersonal relationships and communicating effectively.

Analysis of how body language is used for manipulation

As we've seen, body language can be used in manipulative ways in various ways. For example, maintaining constant eye contact can be used to make a message seem more convincing but also to intimidate the listener. Using exaggerated gestures can emphasize a point but also manipulate the listener's emotions to make them more inclined to believe the message.

Additionally, how posture is used can be manipulative. A dominant posture, such as crossing arms or assuming a position where one towers over the listener, can be used to intimidate, or manipulate the other person. On the other hand, avoiding eye contact can make a person appear less confident and less credible.

Ambiguous facial expressions can also be used to confuse or manipulate the listener. For example, a fake smile can be used to make it seem like something positive is being said when in reality, something negative is intended. Changing the tone of voice can also influence the listener's perception of the credibility and authority of the speaker.

However, it's important to note that body language can be used positively and negatively. For example, maintaining constant eye contact can convey a sense of security and self-confidence and establish an emotional bond with the other person. Using natural and appropriate gestures can help emphasize a point and make the message clearer. Using facial expressions that match the message being conveyed can help make the message seem more authentic.

Essentially, the way in which body language is used can significantly influence the perception and interpretation of words and messages. Awareness of one's body language and the ability to recognize and resist the manipulation of body language by others can be important for communicating effectively and authentically and avoiding manipulating others or being manipulated.

In general,, being aware of one's body language and its impact on communication can help improve the ability to communicate effectively with others. This requires greater attention to one's posture, gestures, facial expressions, and tone of voice, as well as the ability to recognize and understand the body language of others.

It is important to note that body language is not the only factor that influences communication. Context, culture, relationships, and past experiences can also significantly impact the understanding and interpretation of messages. For example, some gestures and facial expressions may be interpreted differently depending on the country or cultural background. Additionally, the relationship between the people involved can influence the perception of body language. For example, constant eye contact may be seen as reassuring and friendly among friends but too invasive and intimidating in a formal context.

Furthermore, body language does not always correspond to the words spoken. In some cases, people may unconsciously use their body language, revealing their true emotions or intentions. In other cases, people may use their body language intentionally to mask their true emotions or intentions.

Therefore, it is important to pay attention not only to the body language of others but also to the words spoken and the context in which they are spoken. Active listening and the ability to ask relevant questions can help clarify any misunderstandings or inconsistencies between body language and words.

Finally, it is important to note that body language is not an exact science. No universal rules determine the meaning of a particular gesture or facial expression. Multiple factors, including personality, emotional states, context, and culture, influence body language. For this reason, it is important to avoid jumping to conclusions or judging people based on their body language.

In summary, body language is an important component of human communication. It is important to pay attention to one's own body language as well as that of others in order to communicate effectively and authentically. Awareness of body language can also help recognize and resist manipulation by others and avoid manipulating others. However, it is important to note that body language is not the only factor influencing communication and that understanding body language requires attention to context, words, and culture.

Examining manipulative techniques based on nonverbal communication

Manipulation techniques based on nonverbal communication can be categorized into various types. Some of these techniques include eye contact, gestures, posture, facial expressions, and tone of voice.

Eye contact is one of the most common nonverbal manipulation techniques. A person who wants to manipulate their conversation partner can use eye contact to create a sense of intimacy or challenge. For example, constant eye contact can make it seem like the person is trying to build an emotional connection with the other, while intermittent eye contact can make the person appear distracted or disinterested. On the other hand, prolonged, fixed eye contact can be used to intimidate and make the other person uncomfortable.

Gestures can be used to emphasize a point or manipulate the emotions of the conversation partner. For example, a person who wants to manipulate their conversation partner can use exaggerated gestures to make the message seem more important than it actually is. Gestures can also be used to create a sense of familiarity or closeness. For example, touching the other person on the shoulder can make it seem like the person is trying to build an emotional connection with them.

Posture can be used to create a sense of dominance or submission. For example, a person who wants to manipulate their conversation partner can adopt a dominant posture, like crossing their arms to make the other person appear less important. Conversely, a person who wants to manipulate their conversation partner can adopt a submissive posture like bending or hunching over to make the other person appear more important.

Facial expressions can be used to manipulate the emotions of the conversation partner. For example, a fake smile can be used to make the person appear friendly or nice, even though there may be selfish or negative motivations behind it. Facial expressions can also be used to create a sense of empathy or understanding. For instance, a person who wants to manipulate the conversation partner can use a sad facial expression to make the person appear closer to them.

Finally, tone of voice can be used to manipulate the conversation partner. For example, a person who wants to manipulate the conversation partner can use a deep and low tone of voice to make the message appear more important than it actually is. Tone of voice can also be used to create a sense of authority or security. For instance, a person who wants to manipulate the conversation partner can use a calm and confident tone of voice to show that they know exactly what they are doing and have the situation under control.

However, it is important to note that these nonverbal manipulation techniques can be used both positively and negatively. For example, constant eye contact can be used to create a genuine emotional connection, while a dominant posture can be used positively to underscore the person's confidence and ideas.

Moreover, not all people can effectively recognize or use these nonverbal manipulation techniques. Some people may be more susceptible to these techniques than others, depending on their personality, experiences, and cultural background. To avoid being manipulated through nonverbal communication, knowing the techniques and how they work is important. This can help recognize when someone is trying to manipulate the conversation partner and respond appropriately by requesting further information or pausing to think about the situation.

Additionally, it is important to communicate effectively and confidently to express one's thoughts and feelings clearly and directly without being influenced by the nonverbal manipulation techniques of others. This can help build healthier and more authentic relationships with others based on mutual understanding and respect.

Exercise: Identification of manipulation techniques based on nonverbal communication

Here's an example of identifying manipulative techniques based on nonverbal communication in an interaction between two people:

Speaker 1: Hi, how are you doing?

Speaker 2: Good, thanks. (Maintains constant eye contact to create a sense of intimacy)

Speaker 1: I was wondering if you have a minute to discuss this new investment opportunity. Speaker 2: Sure, tell me more. (Assumes a submissive posture by leaning slightly towards Speaker 1 to make it seem like they're more important)

Speaker 1: It's a unique investment opportunity with a guaranteed 10% return in just six months. (Uses a low and deep tone of voice to make it seem like the message is important)

Speaker 2: Wow, that sounds interesting. (Expresses interest with a fake smile)

Speaker 1: Yes, it really is an extraordinary opportunity. (Uses exaggerated gestures to emphasize the point)

Speaker 2: I think I'd like to invest. (Touches the other on the shoulder to create a sense of closeness and emotional connection)

In this example, Speaker 1 uses various nonverbal manipulation techniques to convince Speaker 2 to invest. They use eye contact to create a sense of intimacy and emotional connection, a low tone of voice to make it seem like the message is important, exaggerated gestures to manipulate Speaker 2's emotions, and finally, a touch on the shoulder to create a sense of closeness and emotional connection. Speaker 2, on the other hand, assumes a submissive posture by leaning slightly towards Speaker 1 to make it seem like they're more important and expresses interest with a fake smile.

Another example could be when a person who is trying to manipulate their conversation partner adopts a dominant and open body posture to appear very confident. This person could assume an upright posture, with legs apart and hands on hips, or sit in a relaxed manner but with legs apart. This body posture is intended to give the impression that the person is very confident and has a high degree of self-esteem, which could influence the other person's perception of them and make them more likely to accept their ideas or requests without many questions or resistance.

In summary:

Technique	Description	Example
Eye contact	By maintaining constant eye contact, a person can give the impression that they are trying to create an emotional bond with their conversational partner. In contrast, intermittent eye contact can give the impression that the person is distracted or disinterested.	A person maintains constant eye contact to feel closer to the other person and create a sense of connection.
Gestures	Gestures can be used to emphasize a point or manipulate the interlocutor's emotions.	A person uses excessive gestures to give the impression that the message is more important than it actually is.
Posture	Posture can be used to create a sense of dominance or submission.	A person stands upright and crosses their arms to give the impression that the other person is less important.
Facial expressions	Facial expressions can be used to manipulate the emotions of the interlocutor.	A person uses a fake smile to give the impression that they are friendly or kind, even though they are actually hiding selfish or negative motives.
Tone of voice	The tone of voice can be used to manipulate the interlocutor.	A person uses a low and serious tone of voice to give the impression that the message is more important than it actually is.

Exercise

Technique	Description	Example
Eye contact		
Gestures		
Posture		
Facial expressions		
Tone of voice		

13

Using body language
effectively

Body language is a fundamental element of human communication and can convey meanings and intentions that cannot be expressed by words alone. Using body language effectively requires self-awareness, awareness of others, and the ability to adapt to the situation and the interlocutor.

One of the most important ways to use body language effectively is to maintain eye contact with the interlocutor. Constant eye contact can make it feel like we are paying attention and are interested in the conversation. On the other hand, avoiding eye contact or looking away can make it seem like we are disinterested or hiding something.

Adopting an open posture can make it seem like we are open to dialogue and available to interact with others. Crossing arms or legs, on the other hand, can make it seem like we are closed and defensive. Posture is an important way to express our emotional state and adopting an appropriate posture can help us communicate more effectively.

Gestures are another important way to use body language effectively. Gestures can be used to emphasize a point or underline an idea. However, using them sparingly and adopting gestures appropriate to the situation is important. For example, a too large or exaggerated gesture can seem out of place in a formal conversation.

Facial expressions are another way to effectively use body language. Facial expressions can convey a range of emotions, such as happiness, sadness, anger, or surprise. Using them appropriately can help communicate more effectively. For example, smiling can make it seem like we are happy or satisfied while furrowing the brow can make it seem like we are angry or worried.

Listening attentively and showing interest in what the speaker is saying can make it feel like we are engaged in the conversation and eager to understand their perspective. Additionally, adapting our tone of voice to the situation and the speaker can help us communicate more effectively. Tone of voice can convey different emotions and moods, such as enthusiasm, seriousness, irritation, or concern.

Being aware of our own posture and body language can help us communicate more effectively and also influence the perception others have of us. An upright and confident posture can make it seem like we are confident and competent, while a slouched or unsure posture can make it seem like we are insecure or undecided.

In conclusion, body language is a fundamental aspect of human communication and can influence the perception others to have of us. Using it effectively requires self-awareness, awareness of others, and the ability to adapt to the situation and the speaker. Maintaining eye contact, taking an open posture, using gestures and facial expressions appropriately, listening attentively, and adapting our tone of voice can help us communicate more effectively and create a good impression.

Analysis of body language signals that can improve communication and mutual understanding.

Here is a list of body language signals that can improve communication and mutual understanding:

1. Maintain eye contact: Looking into the eyes of the conversation partner can express attention and interest in the conveyed content. It can also help to perceive facial expressions and understand emotions.

2. Adopt an open body posture: Relaxed and open arms and legs can show that we are available and open for the conversation, ready to listen and dialogue.

3. Use appropriate gestures: Gestures can emphasize a point or underscore an idea but should be used appropriately to the situation and tone of the conversation.

4. Express empathy: Gestures such as nodding or smiling can convey empathy and understanding for what the conversation partner is saying, encouraging them to continue speaking and expressing themselves.

5. Adapt tone of voice: Tone of voice can convey a wide range of emotions and moods and adapting it to the situation and the conversation partner can help to communicate more effectively.

6. Avoid muscle tension: A relaxed and natural body posture can help to avoid muscle tension that can make us look tense and nervous.

7. Use appropriate physical contact: Physical contact can be used to convey empathy and closeness but should be used appropriately and respectfully, such as with a handshake or a light hug.

8. Observe and respond to others: Observing the other person and appropriately responding to their body language signals can help to build mutual understanding and avoid misunderstandings.

9. Avoid distractions: Not getting distracted and not being otherwise occupied during the conversation can show that we are interested and attentive.

10. Be authentic: Using our body language naturally and authentically, rather than trying to deceive or hide emotions, can help to build trust and mutual understanding.

In general, using body language effectively requires self-awareness and awareness of others, adaptability to the situation and the interlocutor, empathy, and authenticity. When these elements are present in communication, body language can become a powerful tool for improving mutual understanding and building meaningful relationships. I have rephrased the recommendations for the use of body language to give them greater importance and attention, enabling everyone to communicate more effectively and understandably.

Exercise: Practicing the use of body language in everyday communication

Here are some practical exercises you can do to improve your ability to use body language in everyday communication:

Exercise	Description
Mirror exercise	Try different facial expressions, gestures, and postures in front of a mirror to observe and improve the impression you convey.
Practicing eye contact	Throughout the day, seek eye contact with different people and hold it for a while to find the right balance between eye contact and occasional glances.
Practicing postures	Observe your posture during the day and adopt an upright and open posture to avoid appearing closed off and defensive.
Practicing gestures	During a conversation with friends and family, use appropriate gestures to emphasize important points, underscore your ideas, and avoid exaggerated or inappropriate gestures.
Practicing facial expressions	During a conversation with others, use appropriate facial expressions to express emotions, such as smiling when happy or raising eyebrows when surprised.

Remember that regular practice is the key to improving your ability to use body language effectively in daily communication.

14

Speech about future opportunities for research in this field and the importance of continuing to develop awareness and resilience to manipulation

Research on dark psychology and manipulation is crucial for understanding how some people exert power and control over others through deception, persuasion, and manipulation. This understanding is essential for preventing and combating manipulation and abuse in many areas of life, including personal relationships, work, and politics. Furthermore, research on black psychology can help develop tools and strategies for coping with and preventing manipulation. For example, training programs can be developed to help people recognize manipulation techniques, strengthen their self-awareness and emotions, and develop their ability to resist pressure.

Future research on dark psychology and manipulation could focus on how these techniques are used in new technologies and social media, where manipulation can be even more subtle and insidious. Additionally, it could be useful to examine cultural differences in the application and understanding of manipulation and black psychology.

Manipulation is a problem that affects many areas of life, from personal and interpersonal relationships to work and politics. Dark psychology is a tool some people use to exert power and control over others through deception, persuasion, and manipulation. Therefore, research in this field is crucial for preventing and combating manipulation and abuse.

One of the main obstacles to preventing and combating manipulation is the lack of awareness and knowledge of this phenomenon. Many people cannot recognize manipulation techniques and become victims without realizing it. Research on black psychology can help raise awareness of this problem and provide people with the tools to defend themselves.

In addition, research on dark psychology can help develop training and education programs to teach people how to recognize and resist manipulation techniques. These programs can be useful not only for people who have been victims of manipulation but also for professionals in careers that require a deep understanding of human psychology, such as psychologists, social workers, teachers, and lawyers.

Research on dark psychology and manipulation could also focus on new technologies and social media, where manipulation can be even more subtle and insidious. For example, many people rely on social media as a source of information and are often exposed to false and manipulative news. Research could examine how manipulation techniques are used on social media and how people can protect themselves from them.

Additionally, research on dark psychology could examine cultural differences in the use and understanding of manipulation. In some cultures, for example, certain manipulation techniques may be more prevalent or accepted than others. Research could examine how these cultural differences affect the understanding of manipulation and how appropriate prevention and combat strategies can be developed for each culture.

Finally, research on dark psychology could help develop public policies to prevent and combat manipulation. For example, authorities could use the knowledge gained from research to develop awareness campaigns and training programs for the prevention of manipulation. In addition, laws could be amended to make reporting and punishing manipulation and abuse easier.

In conclusion, research on dark psychology and manipulation are crucial for understanding how some people seek to exert power and control.

Exercise: Reflection on personal progress in understanding and resilience to manipulation

Reflecting on one's progress in understanding and resilience to manipulation can be an extremely useful process for becoming aware of one's abilities and limitations in this area. To begin, it is important to make an honest and objective assessment of one's knowledge and skills related to manipulation and dark psychology. For example, which manipulation techniques are known, and which are not? How does one distinguish between one's own and others' induced emotions and feelings? What tools and strategies are known for resisting manipulation?

Once the areas in need of improvement have been identified, an action plan can be developed to refine one's skills. Opportunities can be sought to apply this knowledge in real-life situations, such as practicing resilience to manipulation in social or professional situations. After developing these skills, it is important to regularly evaluate one's progress. For example, how well was manipulation recognized and resisted in certain situations? How has one improved differentiating between one's own and others' induced emotions and feelings? How has an awareness of one's vulnerability to manipulation increased, and how has the ability for self-protection developed?

Reflecting on one's progress in understanding and resilience to manipulation can be an ongoing and evolving process. Manipulation is a complex and subtle challenge that requires continuous effort to develop and improve one's skills. However, with practice and dedication, it is possible to become more aware and capable of resisting manipulation and protecting oneself and others.

Here is a possible table for practicing reflection on one's progress in understanding and resilience to manipulation:

Evaluation Area	Reflection Questions	Current Score	Improvement Objectives
Knowledge of Manipulation Techniques	Which manipulation techniques are known, and which are not?	[0-10]	Learn to recognize and distinguish all manipulation techniques
Identification of Own Emotions and Feelings	How do you distinguish your own emotions and feelings from those induced by others?	[0-10]	Increase self-awareness and develop the ability to identify your own emotions and feelings.
Tools and Strategies for Resisting Manipulation	Which tools and strategies are known for resisting manipulation?	[0-10]	Deepen knowledge of techniques and strategies for resisting manipulation
Application of Knowledge in Real Life	How has resistance to manipulation been practiced in real life?	[0-10]	Look for opportunities to apply knowledge in real life
Awareness of Vulnerability to Manipulation	How has an awareness of own vulnerability to manipulation increased?	[0-10]	Develop the ability to protect oneself and increase awareness of own vulnerability.

These are just examples of possible reflection questions and improvement goals, and the table can be customized according to individual needs and preferences. Additionally, the current score can be expressed in various ways, such as a percentage or rating scale. The important thing is to use the table as a tool for reflecting on progress in understanding and resilience against manipulation and developing concrete improvement goals. Before we continue with the exercise, here is a summary of the manipulation techniques:

1. Flattery: This technique involves making compliments and often excessively praising the target for making them feel good and making it easier to accept the manipulator's requests.
2. Isolation: The manipulator tries to isolate the target from other people, often by criticizing or discrediting them, to reduce their sources of support and increase their influence.
3. Shame: This technique involves making the target feel inadequate or inferior in some way to get them to comply with the manipulator's requests to prove that they are worthy.

4. Threat: The manipulator threatens or promises negative consequences if the target does not comply with their requests to get them to give in and avoid the consequences.
5. Gaslighting: This technique involves making the target believe that they are wrong or going crazy, even if they are not, to make them doubt their perception and accept the manipulator's version.
6. Emotional blackmail: The manipulator tries to make the target feel guilty or exploit their emotions to get them to do what they want.
7. Stockholm Syndrome: This technique involves creating a strong emotional bond between the manipulator and the target, often through isolation and coercion, to make the target develop empathy and gratitude towards the manipulator.
8. Leading questions: The manipulator asks questions or provides suggestions that suggest the desired option and give the impression that the target is making the decision themselves.
9. Confusion: The manipulator uses confusion and language manipulation to disorient the target and get them to follow the manipulator's demands to gain clarity.
10. Moving target: The manipulator continuously changes their goal or requirements to confuse the target and get them to comply with the manipulator's demands.
11. Foster dependency: The manipulator tries to create an emotional or material dependence in the target to get them to rely on the manipulator for their needs.
12. Creating dependence: This technique involves offering an immediate reward that leads to greater dependence and loss of autonomy in the long term.
13. Creating confusion: By using complex words, metaphors, or contradictory statements, the manipulator tries to confuse the targeted person and create a state of uncertainty.
14. Simulated empathy: The manipulator can pretend to feel empathy that they actually do not feel to be accepted and gain the trust of others.

15. Using threats: This technique is based on intimidating the targeted person through hidden or explicit threats to put them in danger and gain their consent.
16. Generating guilt: The manipulator may try to involve the targeted person in guilt or responsibility for situations for which they are not actually responsible for gaining their consent.
17. False sense of security: The manipulator can make the targeted person believe they are safe and protected while the intentions are actually different and may lead to negative consequences.
18. Emotional abuse: This technique is based on exploiting the emotions of the targeted person by making them feel inadequate, insecure, or guilty to gain their consent.
19. Reducing the targeted person to an object: This technique uses the targeted person to achieve a personal goal without considering their needs and desires.
20. Belittling others: This technique is based on attacking the image of the other person to reduce their self-esteem and increase one's own power and control.
21. Selective disclosure of information: This technique is based on offering only certain information to influence the manipulated person's perception of a particular situation.

It is important to be aware of these techniques to be able to recognize and resist them.

Exercise

Evaluation Area	Reflection Questions	Current Score	Improvement Objectives
Knowledge of Manipulation Techniques			
Identification of Own Emotions and Feelings			
Tools and Strategies for Resisting Manipulation			
Application of Knowledge in Real Life			
Awareness of Vulnerability to Manipulation			

Disclaimer

This book contains opinions and ideas of the author and intends to provide helpful and informative knowledge to people. The strategies contained may not fit every reader, and there is no guarantee that they will work for everyone. The use of this book is explicitly at one's own risk. Claims for damages of a material or non-material nature caused by the use or non-use of the information or using incorrect and/or incomplete information are expressly excluded against the author. The author does not guarantee the timeliness, correctness, completeness, and quality of the provided information. Printing errors and misinformation cannot be completely excluded.

Printed in Great Britain
by Amazon

20545011R00071